D1479764

The Bubba Does TEXAS Cookbook with Jokes

by Diane Gregg
Illustrated by Chris Mostyn and Diane Gregg

The second in a Series of

S.O.B. COOKBOOKS

(Sweet Ole Bubba)

A hysterically historical cookbook about Texas;
the way it was, the way it is, the way it always will be.
Hey, it's Texas!

*A collection of over 235 recipes that will knock your socks off while it
has you laughing your head off.*

Title: The Bubba Does Texas Cookbook
         (Number 2 in the Series)

Author: Diane Gregg

Illustrations by: Chris Mostyn and Diane Gregg

Copyright © 1998

First Printing: Oct. 1998; 10,000 copies

Published in the USA
by Diane Gregg
All rights reserved.

Printed by: Hart Graphics, Inc.
             Austin, Texas

ISBN 0-9641380-3-4

★

Dedication

I am dedicating this book in memory of Cynthia Smith, my friend. Although Cynthia was unable to contribute even one recipe, she was in her own way responsible for my writing this sequel. I know she's looking down and saying, "I can't believe it; she actually did what I asked her to do for me."

Thank you, Cynthia.

Illustrated by Chris Mostyn and Diane Gregg

Chris Mostyn illustrated the front and back covers for me again. I think he is so talented. Unfortunately Chris' and my scheduling didn't mesh this time and he could not illustrate the inside of this book. Very unfortunate! I want to thank Chris for doing such a fine job. I feel that he truly captured "Bubba' again as well as "Cowboy." Chris' mother, my very best friend for three decades, has been going shopping without me because I've been so busy writing this book and all it entails. Well, Laura, I'm almost ready to hit the malls! Thanks again, Chris, for a job well done.

The Mangy Range

Home, home on the range
Home to armadillos and dogs with mange
We're Texans ever so proud
Rude, rowdy and pretty loud

We're arrogant and braggadocios
Some of us quite atrocious
There are ladies and gentlemen too
But unfortunately, all too few.

We love to Texas two step
And we do it with a lot of pep
Texans drink a lot of beer
And also hunt a bunch of deer.

Wouldn't be caught dead without our boots
And we never roam too far from our roots
Texans do travel once in a while
But Texas beats every other place by a country mile!

We love to party, drink and eat
Our kinda food just can't be beat
We eat our chicken fried steak
And we picnic by some big ole lake.

We're Texans through and through
No other place will ever do
Here we're born and here we'll die
With a beer in one hand and mud in your eye!

Table of Contents

★

Introduction

When I wrote the Bubba Cookbook with Jokes, I decided to play down my Texas connection. Boy, did I goof! Texas just cannot be down-played. I went to great lengths not to mention Texas on the cover or in the book. I had studied Bubbas for so long that I wanted the emphasis on Bubba, not on Texas. Well, it didn't matter what I wanted because the book just screamed "TEXAS" (Michener, eat your heart out!) After much deliberation, I realized that I personify Texas, as I am Texan, born and bred. While I love to travel, I am like a horse too long away from the barn. The closer I am in proximity to Texas after being away on a trip, the faster I run home to the Lone Star State. Home for me is truly "deep in the heart" as I reside in Austin, very close to the exact center of Texas. What more could one want than to live smack dab in the middle of such a big, beautiful, bountiful state? It's Heaven on Earth.

I got to stay home while writing this cookbook, as I sent Bubba all over Texas gathering information for me. He agreed to help me with the Bubba Does Texas Cookbook because I believe he had just seen "Debbie Does Dallas" and was eager to help. Bubba got such a kick out of driving all over Texas – he has taken to travel like a rat to velcro. In fact, he plans for us to write three more cookbooks together. Of course, that means three more extensive and expensive trips for Bubba. He has gained 40 pounds! He's eaten tons of chicken fried steaks, burgers, Mexican food, and he has never turned down a dessert. He has drunk gallons and gallons of iced tea and beer (when he hasn't been driving, of course). His waist size has gone from a 34 to a 40 while I have been writing this book. He says that's proof he worked really hard. He's on a diet now while we are in between books – a liquid diet. BEER!! I'm sure he'll be back to normal shortly, whatever normal is for him! You know, I gave him my credit card for all his travel expenses, so I'd better check on that. Bubba might have given "shop 'til you drop" a whole new meaning.

It was so easy for me to talk about Texas and Texans, our likes and dislikes, etc. After all, it's what I know. I didn't have to study a thing! I could write this cookbook from my own perspective. I'm still convinced that we all have a little

Bubba or Bubbette in us. Bubbas and cowboys have always gotten along well together in Texas. They sort of blend together just fine. I would like to thank Bubba for doing all my research. I would like to thank cowboys all over Texas for inspiration and thanks to my family once again for giving opinions on the new recipes. My daughters still tell everyone "at our house we pray after we eat" because Mom is always testing, testing, testing! I tell them they look pretty healthy to me!

In the back of this book you can order not only additional cookbooks, but you can order Texas Tees, Bubba and Texas caps and my own Texas Rub Tub – a Texas dry rub for your barbecue. Thanks, Ya'll. I hope to see you again real soon wherever Bubba and I write our next cookbook. Actually, we know the location already and you're going to love it!

Everything in Texas is BIG

Texas flies are so big they are often seen on radar screens and shot down as foreign planes.

Our fire hydrants in Texas are so big that stools are provided for dogs.

Texas jackrabbits are so big that most outsiders think they're furry kangaroos without pockets.

Texas worms are about two feet long so that they can catch those 500 lb. catfish.

The stars are so big and bright in Texas that Texans have to wear sunglasses at night.

Texas gnats are so huge they can be saddled and used for transportation in a pinch.

Texas "horny" toads are so big they are often used in movies as stand-ins for dinosaurs.

Just 4 or 5 Texas fire flies in a jar can light up Dallas.

Texas has such big rivers they would have made Moses think twice.

Texas mosquitoes are so big they try to mate with turkeys.

Cute little BIG story. . .

Two Texas cowboys were fishing off an isolated bridge and drinking beer. They were both a little "too relaxed" to get up when nature called. So, after making sure they were alone, they proceeded to relieve themselves right there. Greatly relieved, the first cowboy said, "Water sure is cold." About a minute later, the second cowboy looked at the first cowboy and said, "Deep too."

My mother hoped you wouldn't read this far. She told me if I included this cute little BIG story, she wouldn't speak to me. It has worked out well!

"Cowboy"

(Rural, not urban, please!)

When I wrote *The Bubba Cookbook with Jokes*, I thought I might have trouble acquainting you with Bubba. I had to acquaint myself with Bubbas for over two years before I felt comfortable enough to write about them. I've decided that Cowboy was easier to describe comparatively speaking. After all, it's what I know. I hope I haven't lived in Texas for all these years for nuttin'!

The dictionary is always my first source of information, and the dictionary states "a cowboy is a ranch worker who rides horseback on his job of herding cattle, or a performer in a rodeo." While that defines cowboy in the strictest sense, it doesn't give you the "feel" of the true Texas cowboy – the spirit of the cowboy is missing. Cowboys come in all sizes, colors and shapes. They speak many different languages as well. A cowboy's work goes on seven days a week, 24 hours a day, and so does he.

Let's dispense with the Rexall Ranger, or drug store cowboy, first. All over Texas there are men running around dressed like a cowboy and driving their pickups they only use on dates. They're "wanna be" cowboys. Most of them couldn't walk and chew at the same time, let alone rope, ride and spit all at once. They're so green they don't even know not to spit into the wind or not to squat with their spurs on. Actually, most of them don't go so far as to wear spurs and chaps, thank goodness! Almost every little boy and girl who grows up in Texas wants to be a cowboy or cowgirl, but most outgrow it unless they are really serious about it. We have little Annie Oakleys and Roy Rogers' all over the place. About the time girls find boys, they give up horses. Boys who are not predisposed to ranch life consider it really hard work to be a cowboy and thus forget it.

Let's get to the real Texas cowboy. He's strong, proud, gentlemanly, patriotic and dedicated – the salt of the earth. Does John Wayne come to mind here, or what? Can't you just see him riding the range, mending fences, branding cattle, chasing the strays, camping out under the stars, shooting rattlesnakes, roping calves, kissing his horse, etc. You get the picture. Personally, I envision George

Strait doing all these things, as I believe him to be a true Texas cowboy and boy, can he sing! He is my ideal cowboy and my hero. I'll bet you a chicken fried steak he can rope with the best of them. He's Texan through and through. You know that old saying, "He can put his boots under my bed anytime!"

I've always thought John Wayne, Roy Rogers and Will Rogers were transplanted Texans. They should have been Texans. While we're not often fooled by Rexall Rangers, I believe these three men could have fooled even a true Texan if they had wished to do so.

A cowboy is a dedicated ranch worker who never rests as long as there is work to be done. He is dependable, and so much depends on him. Being a cowboy is hard, hard work, but it is very rewarding. Texans appreciate the cowboy. We respect him. A real cowboy is usually shy and polite. They don't cotton to "women's lib." They tip their hats to ladies and are generally well mannered. The flip side of this coin is I wouldn't care to make a cowboy mad. They don't "push" well and they don't "corner" at all. They are fiercely loyal. Cowboys are genuine, responsible human beings. There are many great Texas cowboys from the past, present and future. We salute you one and all!

Texas Fried

(Better known as "Grease," but that title is taken)

Texans have hearty appetites when served our own Texas foods. Our appetites drop off dramatically when served other fare. Texas food is as distinguishable and discernable as Texas itself. The staple foods that Texans love, and you might not have all of them in your neck of the woods, are: chicken fried steak with cream gravy, chicken fried chicken with gravy on the side, fried catfish and hushpuppies, burgers and fries, enchiladas, fried okra, chilis and stews with cornbread, big messy sandwiches, tons of potatoes, gallons of beans, cream corn, pork chops, meatloaf, tacos, barbecue, pecan pie, burritos, biscuits, beautiful steaks, cobbler, smothered steak, cornbread dressing, homemade ice cream, pecan pralines, chicken and dumplings, ham, buttermilk pie, macaroni and cheese, salsa by the bucketsful, big moist cakes, homemade rolls, banana pudding. Texas sized cookies, watermelon, roast beef, ranch dressing and black-eyed peas for good luck! Toothpicks all around, ya'll.

Beer is the Texas state drink with iced tea running a close second. If you want hot tea, it will probably come microwaved. We're just not big hot tea drinkers even though I'm sure we consume more tea than people in any other state. We do it by drinking iced tea summer and winter alike. Every restaurant, large or small, sells a disproportionately larger amount of iced tea and beer to their food sales in Texas. Beer is big business and Texas is the only state I've seen where all the beer manufacturers, and I mean the majors, imprint the shape of Texas on cans and bottles or write Texas on them in bold letters. When a Texan drinks a beer, they know they're in Texas. Nearly every restaurant in Texas has neon lights of Texas and beer hanging somewhere and some restaurants have them everywhere! Texans drink their share of soda and coffee too. I might add that the bar business is flourishing as well. Texas has nice bars, sleazy bars, and all in between, but all seem to be doing well.

I believe you could better understand a typical Texas cafe if you view a typical Texas menu. I have chosen a popular menu that you might see anywhere in Texas while driving through.

Welcome To . . .

BUBBA'S
BLUE COLLAR
COUNTRY CLUB CAFE

Somewhere in
TEXAS

OPEN DAILY
11:00 AM-10:00PM

Appetizers
potato skins
buffalo wings
fried mushrooms
queso & chips
chips & salsa

Salads
taco salad
chicken fajita salad
(served with chips)
guacamole
(served with chips)

Mexican Favorites
taco plate
enchilada plate
bowl of chili
(served with tortillas)
Breakfast tacos
served all day

Sides
fries   Onion rings
cole slaw   baked beans
fried okra   pinto beans
pinto beans   potato salad
Mashed potatoes

Bubba's Best
chicken fried steak
chicken fried chicken
fried catfish
fried shrimp
t-bone steak
rib-eye

(includes 2 sides or 1
side & salad &
Texas Toast)

Specialties
southwest chicken breast
baby back ribs
barbecued sausage plate
chopped steak
turkey and dressing (Sun. only)
brisket plate
chicken & dumplings (Sun. only)

(includes 2 sides or 1 side &
salad & Texas toast)

Little Bubbas & Bubbettes
burger
corn dog
chicken strips
chicken fried steak
grilled cheese

(served with 1 side)

Bubba's Burgers
Old Timey burger
Bacon cheese burger
Hickory burger
Jalapeño burger
Mushroom & swiss burger

add cheese   .50
add jalapeños   .50

Sandwiches
club
brisket
ham
turkey
chicken fried steak
grilled chicken breast

(served with 1 side)

Drinks
Iced Tea
sodas
coffee
beer

Desserts
pie   pie a la mode
cobbler   banana pudding
ice cream sundae Fudge brownie

**Thanks. Ya'll come back now!
**In God we trust. All others pay cash.
**Children who misbehave will be sold as short slaves.

The condiments on the table will include salt & pepper, real sugar, ketchup, mustard, steak sauces, and don't forget the Tabasco. Lots of Texans carry this small bottle of fire with them at all times. It travels in purses and pockets.

To be honest, some of the Texas cafes are "greasy spoons" and could just as easily be named "Scarf and Barf," but some of the most nondescript restaurants and cafes serve up some mighty fine Texas fare. You could be lucky and choose what I call a true "Texas grunge" cafe. I know many, many Texas cafes that have original decor from Heaven knows when, none of the "made to look old, newly made stuff." You can see saddles, spurs, Coca-Cola signs, feed sacks, harnesses, biscuit tins, old license plates, barn wood, original light fixtures and very old fans. I know several places that still have hitching posts outside. Heck! I know a few places that still have bathrooms outside! You'll see original wooden floors, ornate bars, maybe some cathedral glass or beveled-leaded glass. These places are all over Texas and we Texans take them for granted, but we do take them! If you can find these places when driving through our fair state, you'll enjoy viewing them and the food will likely be good or the place wouldn't still be there. You'll run into some real cowboys and real Texas Bubbas too. Be sure to say, "Howdy!"

As a rule, Texans have a big appetite for hearty breakfasts. Of course, every household is different and I wouldn't presume to tell you what everyone in Texas has for breakfast, but I can state that most Texans love breakfast and believe that we need a substantial breakfast to start our day off well. We have the traditional Texas breakfasts that might resemble these examples of menus:

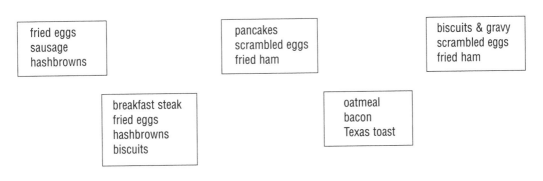

fried eggs
sausage
hashbrowns

pancakes
scrambled eggs
fried ham

biscuits & gravy
scrambled eggs
fried ham

breakfast steak
fried eggs
hashbrowns
biscuits

oatmeal
bacon
Texas toast

One of Texas' most popular breakfast items is the breakfast taco, a whole other category of breakfast food. The breakfast taco is fast, easy, hearty, inexpensive and delicious! It also keeps and travels well. It might just be the perfect breakfast for Texans on the go. You can choose from a variety of flavors, sort of mix and match to suit your AM tastebuds.

First, you start with a hot off the griddle flour tortilla and when cool enough to handle, fill the tortilla with your choice of the following: sausage (I prefer chorizo), bacon, diced potatoes or hashbrowns, grated cheese, scrambled eggs, hot salsa, refried beans, jalapeños. Then, roll it up and eat it. What a great breakfast even if you aren't on the run. I saute my sausage with garlic and onion and some chili powder. Look for the recipe in the book! I know that many people who live in Texas are indignant about my beliefs pertaining to Texas foods, but I don't have a big picture in my head of some cowboy giving up his breakfast taco for a bagel. That dog don't hunt! How about Bubba exchanging his chicken fried steak for crepes? Yeah, right!

Grits in Texas are optional, I don't care what any one says. I've lived in Texas all my life and "this ain't my first rodeo," as we Texans say. No one in Texas has ever offered me grits but once in my whole life and I am as old as dirt (well, almost)! I consider grits more a "deep south" dish.

Texas has all the "chain" burger joints, plus a few you've probably never heard of. Texas is so big, a Texas chain could have 200-300 restaurants and never leave Texas. I believe Texas has more local chains than most states and I believe they are usually superior. If they aren't great, they aren't around very long – there's too much competition. Texans are very serious about their burgers – no small patty without the works for us~! What most Texans envision as their perfect burger is a big, messy, juicy, hot charred patty in a grilled bun with all the trimmings, and a big slice of melted cheese is included. Do not put ketchup on a Texan's burger. Just hold it! Most Texans won't eat a burger with ketchup on it. Ketchup is for fries, and don't call them French fries! We Texans don't like very much French, don't you know? Most Texas males still whisper "mayonnaise" when ordering it on a burger. Until about 20 years ago, Texas waitresses screamed, "Sissy burger" when someone ordered no onions, and mayo as opposed to mustard. It always seemed to me that the scream was a little louder when some macho male ordered mayo than when a female did. It came the closest to making a cowboy faint than anything else I've seen. Cowboys can doctor wormy cows, brand cattle, kill rattlesnakes, be thrown by horses, etc., but they don't want to be associated with a "Sissy burger." They would rather starve. Most of those waitresses have died off now. I sometimes wonder if they had natural deaths or if some cowboy strangled them. The next time you hear a Texan whisper "mayonnaise," you'll know the threat of a "Sissy burger" persists today.

Most Texans like veggies on their burgers, and onions, pickles, and jalapeños are cowboy veggies. We also love barbecue sauce on our burgers, making it a hickory burger. Bacon is nice on most burgers. So is chili, making it a chili burger. We're not shy about onions, and cheese is a must. Fries are a given unless we opt for fried onion rings instead. Huge rounds of onions are individually breaded and deep fried. Are you beginning to realize that Texans like fried foods? I grew up wondering if Texans comprehend boiling, broiling and baking. We comprehend alright, we just like grease! I understand it. I am a Texan! Texans eat more than their share of greasy foods. I do believe you could squeeze any one of us and fry donuts!

Barbecue is a religion in Texas. There are barbecue joints everywhere, and everyone has his or her favorite. I don't know if all Texans are like me, but I have a favorite barbecue restaurant for ribs, another for potato salad, another for beans, etc., etc. I've only known one barbecue restaurant with everything prepared to suit my tastebuds, and I owned it! All the recipes were mine. No wonder I loved it! Let me tell you what to look for in a barbecue restaurant. Meat is paramount. It is just as easy to purchase quality meaty meat as it is to purchase a rib with little or no meat. So, the first thing you look for is a restaurant with a sharp purchaser of meat, plus one who knows how to smoke and flavor meats. I like brisket that is slow cooked and fully smoked for 10-14 hours. I heavily dry rub my briskets and medium dry rub the rest of the meats. The sliced brisket should be tested for tenderness and juiciness. My method is to put a very warm slice from the pit brisket over my index finger. If it falls over my finger forming an upside-down "U," and juices drip down my finger, it is ready. If the meat does not fall over the finger, or there is no juice, the meat is tough or overcooked and dry. No amount of sauce, in my opinion, can repair that. But I am a perfectionist and I love the barbecue business, so I'm very particular. Ribs should be very meaty, juicy, tender and almost falling off the bone. Sausage can be purchased fully cooked so I only leave it in the pit for 25-40 minutes depending on temperature of pit and what else is cooking in there. Good, not too greasy, sausage can be found.

Let's talk for a minute about your old Texas barbecue men, the pit meisters – talk about characters! I've never met a one of them who didn't think that they personally invented barbecue and everyone else is just copying them. That's the truth! A Texas barbecue man would rather eat dirt than acknowledge a woman in the barbecue business or that a woman can barbecue. Horsefeathers! There are definite differences in men and women in barbecue, in my opinion. For example, most of the men (not all) do the following. They buy their potato salad in a large tub and add a little mustard to it. They use bought cole slaw. They do usually make their own pinto beans – same pot, same beans for a week! They open a can of pudding, stick cookies in it and call it banana pudding. And their sauce is usually doctored store bought sauce, mostly the same brand used by men I've noticed! Women tend to use scratch recipes and are a lot neater and cleaner, comparatively speaking. I've been a little rough on these old barbecue men, but not nearly as rough as they can be on women in the business. So, clean up your act guys, and move over – we women are doing barbecue and doing it well.

Besides the meats, we have the sauce to talk about. My sauce is tomato based, thick, hot and slightly sweet. There are those who like it thin and hot, hot. Let's not be lazy. How hard is it to provide both? In your own home or in a restaurant this is a simple thing to do. Make up large batches of both because barbecue sauce stores in the refrigerator very well – like ketchup. It doesn't tend to spoil.

Potato salad and cole slaw should be exceptional and made from scratch. The beans must be very tasty. I recommend both pinto and baked beans as a great choice. It doesn't hurt a barbecue restaurant to have the best peach cobbler, pecan pie and banana pudding in town either!

Barbecue plates and sandwiches, sliced or chopped, are big, big business in Texas. You'll find large, pretentious barbecue restaurants that are pricey – some worth it, some not. You'll find the little holes in the wall all over Texas that serve nothing but barbecue. There is so much competition in barbecue in Texas that it keeps people on their toes and that is a good thing because Texans need barbecue like they need air. You can bet the ranch on that!

Texans also need their Tex-Mex. I grew up with Texas Mexican food as a regular part of my diet – I thought everyone did! In Texas, we eat mostly what we call Tex-Mex, which is a Texas style of cooking Mexican food as opposed to "interior" Mexican food that is not as popular or plentiful in Texas.

Tex-Mex is a good use of ground meats, used to make chili con carne, which is used in so many Mexican foods. The meat is simmered with hot Mexican seasonings, long and low, until the meat and spices blend together to make the most delicious chili to be poured over enchiladas, tamales or even over rice and beans for a simple taste treat, especially when topped with chopped onions and grated cheese. Yummy! Add warm tortillas to this dish and it's double yummy. You'll be as happy as a dead pig in the sunshine with this.

Texas has such an expansive border with Mexico, giving us a huge, I mean huge, Mexican influence on our food in Texas. We have other influences such as German, etc., but nothing to compare to the Mexican influence. Texas has a Mexican restaurant every few blocks. You can't miss it! Most of them are full – full of cowboys and Bubbas too. Say, "Howdy."

If you've never lived where you can run down to Mexico to shop, eat and just have fun for a few days whenever you like, you've missed something. It is so much fun to head south of the border for great Mexican food, mariachis, margaritas, etc. It's a good place to relax. I like to go to Laredo. Yes, the Cadillac Bar is still going strong! So is the Moderno in Piedras Negras. All the border towns have some good shopping and at least one or two good restaurants and bars.

Texans just love hunting and fishing. Texas has a large supply of fish in our many, many rivers and lakes. Most Texans are wild about fishing. Texans do love seafood, but those who don't live near the coast are more limited in their selection. Texas has great seafood on our coasts and we love to go to the beach. The Third Coast, as it is called, is where Texans love to go to play in the sand and eat our share of fresh seafood. Close to Louisiana, there is a strong Cajun influence, and because Texans love hot food, we took to Cajun like "white on rice." I especially like the seafood restaurants that serve family style so that you can sample a little of everything.

I can't forget that Texas has more Chinese restaurants than China. It is mind boggling to see a Chinese restaurant in nearly every block. Texans must be buying an awful lot of chinese food. My personal thought on this is that they reached the cowboys and Bubbas when nearly all of the Chinese restaurants installed an "all you can eat" buffet for lunch, and many of them run through dinner. This appealed to Texans, evidently.

Texas women used to know how to ring a chicken's neck and fry it for dinner along with all their other many chores. Now we are inundated with fried chicken franchises and I say, "Thank the Lord!" If it had been up to me to ring a chicken's neck, we'd eat more possum. If it had been up to me, I wouldn't even be a Texan – I'd still be at Plymouth Rock. My wagon would have needed air conditioning and color t.v. or I would not have come to Texas! Then I could have had a bumper sticker that said, "I wasn't born in Texas, but I got here as soon as I could." But I was born here. I'm true BIT. That's what I call a "born in Texas" kind of person!

Texas is just filled with every kind of restaurant anyone could wish for. We also have great supermarkets. Food in general is very good and plentiful in Texas. If you want to cook yourself, you're set. If you want to drive thru and get fast food, you're set. If you want to leave the kids at home and dress to the nines, you're set. Whatever floats your boat, you'll find in the Lone Star State. Bon appetit, ya'll!

Texas

A southwest state of the United States situated on the Gulf of Mexico and the Mexican border, some 267,339 square miles, or so the dictionary says, but what the dictionary does not say . . .

Texas is just one big metaphor! It's said that Texas is more a state of mind than a state. There is a spirit here in the Lone Star State that is unmatched by any other ten states put together. Texas is an intensely vibrant state that is bigger than life. It's like a runaway train filled with all the treasures life has to offer and you're aboard. Texas is on the move!

There are so many things that make Texas Texas – the unique shape, the shear size and I could go on and on, but the number one thing that makes Texas Texas is it's people. Texans are a fine mix of Anglo, Hispanic, German, African American, Swede and to a lesser degree, everything else you can think of! There is a good, hearty mix, a nice blend of strong people working together for the betterment of themselves, their families, their country and Texas, always Texas. Texans are diverse but come together to get the job done. Texans have served 6 flags and served them well. We're a flag waving bunch here. Our flag is red, white and blue – red for courage, blue for loyalty and white for liberty. Texans take their flag seriously. We take our state seriously. I believe you could kidnap and blindfold someone who is totally unfamiliar with Texas and parachute them from a plane into any city or town in Texas and they would know instantly upon removing the blindfold exactly where they were. The imprint of Texas is everywhere. It's on nearly every business, or the business is named Texas Chevrolet, Lone Star Computers, Deep in the Heart Pools, Tejas Trailers, etc. I suspect we paint TEXAS on rooftops for planes to see! We have a pride in Texas that is unmatched anywhere. The Texas name or imprint is on beer bottles, beer cans, napkins, cups, billboards, menus, license plates, signs, books, even toilet paper.

Texas is a sprawling, rip roaring state, a virtual beehive of energy. It has a life all its own. There's nothing stale about Texas because it is constantly renewing itself.

Foreigners (anyone not from Texas) think of Texans as braggadocios and loud – Loud, maybe, even a little squirrely by nature. I agree. But I must tell you it truly is hard to be humble when you're from Texas. It does sound like we're bragging when we talk about Texas to an outsider. Here's why – what don't we have here? Texas has mountains, beaches, plains, valleys, more rivers and lakes than our share, big oil and gas, king cotton, big timber industry, extensive farming and ranching, the Dallas Cowboys, the Dallas Mavericks, the Houston Rockets, the San Antonio Spurs, the Houston Astros, hunting and fishing a plenty, a silicon valley, good schools and universities, friendly hard working people, beautiful scenery, fabulous food, fun shopping, festivals galore, big theme parks, and I could go on forever.

I will agree that politics in Texas is a contact sport. People seem to be about equally split between Republicans and Democrats and never the twain shall meet! There is little ambivalence in Texas politics, folks.

Texas is not a welfare state and you'd better be on your best behavior while you're here. Texans take the law seriously and apply it accordingly. In other words "Don't Mess With Texas" is a serious message to residents and visitors alike.

Texans are great "greeters." You can hear "Howdy, Hidy, Welcome ya'll and Ya'll come" from Lubbock to Laredo. But be wary, you can just as easily hear "Yankee, go home," "Now ya'll go home," "Git the hell outta here" from El Paso to Houston too! This usually means you've just told a Texan how much better something is in the state you live in or you just moved from, that's all. This is a "NO-NO." It would be better to tell a Texan his kids are U-G-L-Y than to criticize Texas, don't you know? For the most part Texans are the friendliest folks on earth, but get them riled up and they can be ornery in the extreme. Remember – (I'll bet you thought I was going to say Remember the Alamo!) not a disparaging word, not about Texas, that is! Of course, Texas has more than it's share of true Texas characters. They're a part of our culture. We just expect to see them and hear them in cafes, post offices, on street corners, in churches, drug stores and just anywhere they can weave a Texas tale. No one can spin a tale the way they can. No one believes half of what they say and question the other half. I must have heard a thousand Texas tales and can't remember them all. Actually most of them I've tried hard to forget! They can tell you about the day old Billy Bob shot the 92 point buck. It was so big it tore the wall down when they tried to hang it. Or how about old George who was chased by the tornado? The only thing that saved him was lightning striking the tornado and splitting it into two tornadoes that went off into different directions. One of the famous food stories, widely told by barbecue men when opening a barbecue restaurant that is not successful from the git-go so it closes within a couple of weeks, goes as follows. "Yeah, I had to close my place down – broke my heart! – Had so many customers the first week the floor just fell in, just fell right in. Health department won't let me reopen. They say it would just happen again. So, I've had the most successful barbecue restaurant in history and I'll just retire from barbecue now while I'm the best. You know, while I'm on top so to speak." Isn't that a hoot? I swear I was told that, I swear. How about the farmer who lived alone and had a heart attack in the barn. He says his pig just cranked up the pickup and drove him to the hospital. Saved his life! One of the tales I enjoyed was an old timer telling me what happened to his friend while the two of them were fishing. It goes like this – Old Jim Ed went 20 miles downstream yesterday. He caught a fish so big it pulled him in and he got caught up in the line and the fish pulled him 20 miles downstream, nearly drowned him! That fish weighed at least 200 pounds, maybe more. One oldtimer got mad at another and put a rattlesnake in his mailbox. The neighbor he got mad at called him and asked him to pick up his mail while he was out of town. He swears he forgot and opened the mailbox to get his neighbor's mail and the snake he put in the mailbox bit him! I really like the 3 headed cow story. The cow would have caused a sensation except for the fact that only one of the heads could talk. Do you see what I mean? It seems everything in Texas is a contest, from telling tales to beer drinking, to pie eating, to barbecuing to just about anything. These characters are a part of Texas culture, plain and simple.

I would like to give you a visual picture of what I see in my mind's eye when I think about Texas. Remember that I live in Austin and will impart that impression to you. I see rolling hills with enormous old oak trees with some mesquite and scrub cedar mixed in. Let's add a stream or creek and a barbed wire fence with a gate. On the rolling hills are so many wildflowers it resembles a colorful quilt. You'll see bluebonnets, Indian paintbrush, milkweed, buttercups, sage and many others. One of the prettiest wild bushes is the Mountain Laurel.

Cactus is beautiful with colorful blooms on it. Now let's throw in some of God's creatures – maybe deer, squirrels, birds and how about an armadillo rooting around. There's probably a water well and windmill close by. I like to see cows licking their calves. Everything is so peaceful and beautiful. This is Texas to me. There isn't anything or anyplace more desirable in our great nation. It has always struck me strange when I've heard someone indicate that all of Texas is flat and dry. Believe me, these statements are born out of ignorance. It would be as silly to say that all of California is desert because someone visited Barstow or Needles and didn't visit beyond! Texas has places that rival San Francisco for hilliness, places that are as lush and green, etc. Texas is such a vast and unique state. I don't mean to sound like the Chamber of Commerce, but I'm Texas proud. Texas truly is like a whole other country, so come on down or over or up, we'll eat some great Texas food, shop some truly Texas shops, sightsee and do a little Texas Two Step or Cotton Eyed Joe. You (not me) can even scream "bull----" if you like. Is this a great state or what? We'll swim in the Gulf of Mexico, run over south of the border and choose from a zillion other things to do. It will be an experience you"ll treasure.

Did I mention that Texas has more stars than any other place on earth? And the moon is larger too! And the sunsets are absolutely breathtaking. I think I'll end this with Texas sunsets, the perfect end to a perfect Texas day.

Bubba says . . .
"Love NY? Take I-35 due north!"

A Texas Lesson on "How to Pick a Prick"

(Shame on you. What a dirty mind you have!)

The prickly pear cactus has long provided Texas cowboys with a toothpick while out on the range. The cactus has many large sturdy thorns on each pear that can be picked off between the thumb and index finger to be used as a disposable toothpick. I first watched this process as a pre-schooler and have always taken the practice for granted where cactus and cowboys come together.

Until I was 12 years old I had several horses and loved to ride. I rode in the parades then sponsored by the Williamson County Sheriff's Posse Association in Georgetown, Texas. I rode every weekend and I believe that every child would enjoy and benefit from the farm and ranch experiences I've known is my early life. I haven't ridden in many years, but I have always missed it throughout my life. I understand the camaraderie between rider and horse. Horses are good company and if you know how to handle them they always agree with you and do your bidding. No wonder cowboys kiss their horses more often than their wives!

I have never taken offense at the title of this lesson. I didn't realize the shady connotation until now. However, reality having set in, I do apologize if you are offended in anyway, (Mother). (Or was that the Huisache?)

Prickly Pear Jelly

Prickly Pear Cactus fruits
3/4 cup sugar per cup of juice
1 tablespoon lemon juice per cup of juice

If some cowboy hasn't removed the thorns to use as toothpicks, do so. Wash and cut into fourths and place in a large saucepan with enough water to barely cover. Slowly cook until fruit is almost pulp. Pour into a jelly bag that has been moistened in hot water. Hang bag over a large bowl overnight to drain. Bring juice to a boil and boil 6 minutes. Remove froth and measure juice. Add 3/4 cup sugar and 1 tablespoon lemon juice for each cup of juice. Cook syrup to 9° above boiling. Pour into sterile jelly jars. Use 1 jelly jar for each cup of juice. Cover with melted paraffin.

★

Texas Talk

(Texas "hoof and mouth" disease)

Texans do love to talk, talk, talk. Just ask anyone of us for directions and you'll be headed in the right direction only after you've answered the proper questions. "Now who are you?" "Why are you going there?" "How long do you plan to stay?" "Just passing through, are you?" It goes on forever. We're a friendly group of people. It's hard to believe anyone could talk so much and still tell the truth. Most Texans are generally more colorful than truthful, but we mean well. We use a lot of Texas oxymorons such as "Hell, he wouldn't be happy if you hung him with a brand new rope!" Check out these examples of "Texas Talk."

doesn't matter – Don't make no never mind.

acceptable – There ya go!; That dog will hunt.

feelin' froggy – Wanna fight?

We'll call before coming over – We'll rattle before we strike.

acquaintance – We've howdied, but never shook.

busy – Busy as a one-legged man at an a_ _ kicking contest.

experience – This ain't his first rodeo.

end of a date – Let's swap spit and hit the road.

braggart – He can strut sittin' down!

independent – Independent as a hog on ice.

unwelcome – As unwelcome as a skunk at a garden party.

stupid – It's better to keep your mouth shut than to open it and remove all doubt.

a Texas toast – Over the lips, over the gums, look out stomach, here it comes.

in a hurry – Hell bent for leather; light a shuck.

squirrely – nuts, crazy.

bad reputation – She looks like she's been rode hard and put away wet.

stealing – Hotter'n a stolen tamale.

unfortunate – She went to the well and the hogs ate her.

big rain – gullywasher.

lack of rain – dry spell.

★

distance – Just a hoot 'n a holler away; down yonder, over yonder.

thirsty – Spittin' cotton.

hungry – I'm so hungry my stomach thinks my throat's been cut.

tired – plumb tuckered out.

legal advice – Never sign nothin' by NEON.

arrival – Well, speak of the devil.

large – Bigger 'n Dallas; he was so big he had to sit down in shifts.

cautious – Love your enemy but keep your gun loaded.

mad at someone – I wouldn't spit on him if he was on fire.

don't care – Don't give a rip; Don't give a rat's rump.

lazy – Call in the dog and see if it's raining.

appreciation – Any time you pass my house I appreciate it.

limp – He's got a hitch in his git-along.

quick exit – Time to get the hell outta Dodge.

heavy traffic – Someone must have left the gate open.

affirmation – Okedoke; You got it; Alrightie then.

climbing the social ladder – Runnin' with the big dogs.

political advice – Don't piss on my leg and tell me it's raining.

obvious – If grandma had cojones she'd be grandpa.

cheap – He's so tight he squeaks when he walks.

really angry – Hang 'em high.

mean – Meaner 'n a junk yard dog.

unsophisticated – country as clabber.

warning – Lie down with dogs and get up with fleas.

negative – Git outta here; No way José, uh uh.

absence – You're a sight for sore eyes.

inebriated – Drunk as a skunk.

fast – Faster 'n a prairie fire with a tailwind.

dumb – If dumb was dirt he'd own a few acres.

ignorant – Doesn't know his a_ _ from a hole in the ground.

bad luck – He's snakebit; If he didn't have bad luck he wouldn't have any luck at all.

poor – He's so poor he couldn't pay attention.

brave – It's better to die on your feet than on your knees.

★

information – If a frog had wings it wouldn't bump it's butt.

Texas advice – There's never been a horse that couldn't be rode; there's never been a cowboy that couldn't be throwed.

ugly – She's as ugly as homemade soap.

celebration – We'll shoot out the lights; Hot damn in the old town tonight.

stupid – He's so stupid he'd screw up a two car funeral.

crazed person – She's a few stitches short of a quilt; He's a couple of beers short of a six pack.

not attractive – Butt ugly.

uneducated person – Doesn't know s_ _ _ from shinola.

right – Damn straight!

dark – Dark as campfire coffee.

happy – Happy as a hog in mud; Yahoo!

not mannerly – raised in a barn.

sad – So sad it would make a Texas Ranger cry.

unorganized – Can't get all your coons up one tree.

There are people who believe that because of our colloqualisms and extremely relaxed speech, Texans are in general ignorant and uneducated. Many of us are exactly that, but the woman you saw schlepping around yesterday might be "all done up" and wearing a rolex, diamonds and furs today. I knew two brothers who bought and sold land all over Texas for 50 years. When they were purchasing they wore overalls and drove a 20 year old pickup. When they were selling they drove a new Cadillac and wore expensive suits. I was as confused as a goat on astroturf after years of watching them operate until I figured out their clever game. It certainly worked for them. Both were college graduates and extremely wealthy, but only on alternate days! You never know about a Texan, but usually the more affluent the Texan, the more low key they are. The "nouveau riche" in any state are irritating, aren't they? If you hear "I've got mine, I've made it big, etc." usually it's followed by "But don't cash my check until next week." That's Texas!

Texans poke fun at other Texans, but never Texas. If referring to someone with big hair you might hear "She has hair like a west Texas waitress." Or "A

Texas attorney is easy to predict, he's only lying if his lips are moving." How about "She's as cold as a Texas banker's heart." I remember an alleged scandal involving someone who stood up at a huge gathering and announced "I'd rather have a sister in a Texas whorehouse than a brother governor of Arkansas." It resulted in a job change – or so the Texas story goes.

Texans have more stories than you can shake a stick at. We speak in Texaseze. Aw, shucks, I'm sure you git my drift! Pert near anyhow. I'm fixin' to tell you that rural Texans speak this way more than those raised on concrete. It keeps us close to our Lone Star roots, I reckon. I'm sure we'll howdy again the good Lord willin' and the creeks don't rise. For now it's time to put out the fire, call in the dogs and outten the lights on Texas talk. Say "Hello" to your mama and them. Ya'll come back now, ya hear?"

This & That In Texas

(Using the F word constantly)

I'm warning you now – I'm going to be using the "F" word a lot in this cookbook – FOOD! It's the only F word I use and I use it constantly. Everything in Texas, and I mean everything, is done with and around Food. We eat our way through every circumstance. When someone is born we take Food. Every meeting, ceremony and gathering has Food. Every wedding reception, graduation and shower has Food. If the churches didn't offer those great covered dish suppers they'd lose more than a few sinners, I'm afraid. Texans can eat and play cards at the same time. We can darned sure drive and eat at the same time. I told you in The Bubba Cookbook with Jokes that I can eat and give birth at the same time! We eat indoors, we eat outdoors, we eat in the air, we just eat, eat, eat. But the real biggie as far as Food is concerned in Texas is the Funeral Food – it gets a double F. I swear it's almost worth it to drop dead for all the delicious and abundant Food that is brought forth. I've never witnessed such a recipe swapping frenzy in my life! Why the body isn't even cold and every oven in town has Food in it to take to the home of the deceased. You can hear stock comments as "Shame Leroy isn't here to enjoy this, I made his favorite." Good Lord! In Texas Food rules. Just look at all the F words.

There are lots of things I don't understand about Texas to this day, even after all these many years here. I'll share a few of them. Naturally I've never understood some of our souvenir items that have Texas written all over them such as tarantulas and scorpions in a bottle or encased in plastic. I don't care for the rattles off a rattlesnake or the snake skin either. How about those stuffed armadillos playing cards and drinking beer? That reminds me of something I'm concerned about. I've noticed taxidermy shops springing up everywhere in Texas. I didn't know Texans had such fascination for stuffing things. I've been in several homes with trophy-type bucks and fish, but nothing that would account for all the new taxidermy shops. I'm afraid there's a conspiracy to start stuffing people and sending them home to sit on the sofa instead of burying them. Maybe the funeral homes are slowly going out of business – I do know the taxidermy shops are gaining on them!

★

Texas is big on laundromats and cafeterias, but most Texans refer to them as washaterias. We're just washateria and cafeteria crazy. I must admit that we have some pretty decent cafeterias in the Lone Star State. They're clean, attractive and certainly convenient. They have their place.

Texans love their courthouses. We're just courthouse people. Most towns and county seats with a courthouse keep them in pristine condition and they are the focal point of the community. Georgetown is a perfect example of having a lovely old courthouse and nice shopping and visiting places all around the courthouse square. It looks much the same as it did when I was growing up there and I always enjoy going back to visit. Georgetown reminds me of another thing we Texans just take for granted. We have large, wonderful, well cared for public parks. The San Gabriel Park in Georgetown is a great example. I still drop by there when I'm traveling I-35 and have a few minutes to spare. I love to stroll along the river and I still swing, but not out over the river anymore! Our parks are such community assets and enjoyed by all.

In my opinion, Texas doesn't provide enough post offices and not enough mail drops by half. You can use half a tank of gas trying to mail a letter. Just a couple of decades ago in Texas the post office was the "happening" place. So many people received their mail at the post office as opposed to home delivery just to visit with their friends and acquaintances every day, and I mean every day, but Sunday. I was in the fourth or fifth grade before I realized that we could have used that hour every day for another purpose! That was the way it was back then in Texas. The mailmen read your postcards. They knew when you were expecting a letter or owed a past due bill I suspect. The only solution I can offer is a proposal to merge the post offices with the IRS and we'll never hear from either of them again! It would be sorta like sending that sock to "Sock Heaven." Every time I do a large load of underwear I lose a sock. I'm sure you do too; I can't be the only one! After searching for hours I finally give up and say "OK, that sock went to 'Sock Heaven'"!

We've talked a lot about our great Texas guys, but not much has been said about our Texas ladies. Texas produces terrific women. We come in all shapes and sizes, all hair colors, all educational backgrounds, all heritages, but we're all Texas ladies and Texas proud. We're raising our children and grandchildren to be the next generation of strong Texans and to appreciate their proud heritage as well.

★

Texas women are cute, smart, savvy and pretty as a picture! Texas ladies are good mothers and wives and caring daughters and granddaughters and best friends.

Many people think that Texans still wander dirt streets wearing six shooters having shoot outs at high noon over serious matters. Nonsense! Texans use concealed guns to settle trivial disagreements on concrete and usually at night. Now that I've cleared that up . . . we're not really the wild, wild west. We're the wild and crazy southwest growing like a bad weed. People are flocking to Texas from everywhere. We have a saying here – "Someone must have left the gate open" and it certainly applies.

Texas has some very funny politicians and political writers. Oddly enough they're nearly all Democrats. I've wondered for years if Texas Republicans lack a sense of humor. I've also wondered why the Democrats don't realize that they would be so much funnier if we didn't know their political persuasion and it would certainly benefit them as they would have double the material to work with if they made fun of fellow Democrats as well as Republicans. I've decided they would rather be half as funny than to crack a joke about one of their own. In Texas we have what we refer to as "yellow dog Democrats." It means the Democrats would vote for a yellow dog before they would vote for a Republican. It's true, it's true, I swear. Ann Richards and Molly Ivins are a hoot to be sure, but so are the George Bushes, younger and older alike. They're pure Texas! All of them. Another Texas first lady, besides Barbara Bush, to be proud of is Ladybird Johnson who has been faithfully dedicated to the beautification of our highways and byways.

Texans start their children off at an early age (around 6 months) to be athletically competitive so that they (the parents) may be allowed to make complete fools of themselves on the sidelines or in the bleachers of any and all games until all their children graduate. I would love to see two things happen. First I would like to see the parents out on the field playing their hearts out and the kids yelling their heads off and making nincompoops of themselves just once. Secondly I would like to know that all those parents are cheering just as loudly for their children's grades. High school sports are huge in Texas and I'm glad the parents are supportive as I was of my kids. Texans do get a little rambunctious and rowdy at athletic events – that's because we're so good! Texas produces good athletes. Then we lose them to other states.

★

We Texans talk a lot about the weather. Someone said "Texas doesn't have seasons, just weather." I agree. The joke here is "If you don't like the weather in Texas, just wait a minute." I agree with that too. The weather is unpredictable here. A "Blue Norther" can come from nowhere and the temperature can drop 30 degrees in minutes or the temperature can be unbearably and unseasonably hot. We can, however, predict with certainty that from about June 15th through September 15th we are going to be HOT! July and August are extremely hot. Other than for about 3 months out of each year Texas weather is very good. Texas attracts golfers, swimmers and tennis buffs due to the good weather. Long ago I read where someone said "If I owned Texas and hell, I'd rent out Texas and live in hell." He must have been here during July and August!

I have to mention the Dallas Cowboys, you know. They've had their ups and downs, but Texans love them. They're our team. Go Cowboys!

Lets talk about horse trading. Texans are great horse traders from a way back. This has spawned many jokes such as "Why, he'd sell his grandmother if they threw in a six pack." There are many old horse traders who swap for a living and never work at any other vocation their whole lives. They're very good at it. Most people tend to stay away from them for fear of losing their underwear. Another popular vocation in Texas is to sell a small business that is hard work and not too profitable and then buying it back for a lesser price than you sold it for. If you do it enough times you can get rich off a small business that is less than desirable. I know an owner of a theater, a drug store owner and many restaurant owners who have done very well doing this exact thing. We trade cars, food, horses, wives – just anything when we can make a buck! Horse traders will be in Texas as long as there is a Texas. Long live Texas!

There is lots of talk about "roadkill" in Texas. I hear it all the time and always have. It's just another of those many Texas things I don't understand. I've never known anyone to eat roadkill in Texas, but I don't claim to know everyone in Texas or what they eat. I expect to see a "Roadkill Grill" opening any day.

Texans just love to have fun, another F word. Food and Fun are a big part of the Texas experience. I'm glad I live here. Life is so good in the Lone Star State. It's predictably good. It's because we demand and expect it in every small town and big city throughout Texas. Remember that all our good times in Texas involve the F word – Food! (and beer)

★

Nowhere But Texas!

You can find some of these things in most states, most of these things in some states, but only in Texas can you find all of these things!

10 gallon hats & Laundromats
West Texas wind & Big Bend
Rio Grande & Padre sand
yellow rose & cotton-eyed Joes
chaps & caps
denim & venom
boots & coots
pits & spits
beans & jeans
deer & beer
high teas & dungarees
wind mills & Sam Hills
longhorns & longnecks
Stetsons & Texans
moos & booze
picture shows & dominoes
oak & poke
spurs & burrs
musicians & politicians
feed & seed
big skies & moon pies
pesos & quesos
waterfalls & overalls
whistles & thistles
football & "Howdy Ya'll"
heat & mesquite
guitars & Cadillacs

possom & poker
trash & cash
boats & goats
cowboys & cactus
buns & guns
Bit Tex & Tex-Mex
Bubbas & Bubbettes
catfish & covered dish
hookers & cookers
bluebonnets & Shakespearean sonnets
debutantes & restaurants
tornadoes & tattoos
denim & diamonds
nuts & sluts
dust & lust
State Fair & big hair
old oaks & friendly folks
smokes & jokes
southern drawls & barroom brawls
microchips & queso dips
hummingbirds & computer nerds
college dorms & thunderstorms
amusement parks & border narcs
big fleas & pecan trees
trailers & hay bailers
schools & pools
singers & swingers

★

cow patties & sugar daddies

Amarillos & armadillos

pride & hide

stars & bars

courthouses & outhouses

barbecue & "Howdy do"

steaks & lakes

chivalrous gents & fender dents

ropes & dopes

neon & northers

studs & duds

rodeos & roadkill

hunks & punks

horned frogs & junk yard dogs

fried pies & Dixie pride

dusty roads & big old toads

beauty queens & Lean Cuisines

cowboys & expensive toys

saddles & battles

bake sales & hay bales

Sunday go to meetings & friendly greetings

oil rigs & shindigs

bats & cats

riverwalks & mules that balk

oil & royal

horses & golf courses

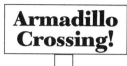

The armadillo is the Texas State mascot! Allow me to share a little history of the armadillo, as I researched it for a children's book I wrote several years ago.

The armadillo is seen all over the state of Texas, especially in rural areas. It is a burrowing, hard shelled mammal that is grayish-taupe in color. The Texas armadillo has nine bands across it's back that move so the armadillo has flexibility. The armadillo has cute, pointy little ears and a nose somewhat like a small anteater.

When in danger, the armadillo quickly digs a hole and crawls into it. If there is no time in which to burrow, the armadillo just sits down and pulls his legs up and his head and tail into his shell, providing him with a kind of armor to protect himself.

Armadillos are chiefly nocturnal, so they love to roam the wide open spaces by night because the moon is bigger in Texas and because we have so many stars. The moonlight just pours down on the armadillos as they roam and gather the vegetation they need for their survival.

The armadillos migrated up from the South and Central Americas, and when they found Texas, they knew they were home! There are no Yankee armadillos that I know of.

Oh, they had to survive a few armadillo jokes such as, "Armadillos are just o'possum on the half shell." But endure these jokes they have. Texans really love their armadillos and always brake for them. Texas is a natural habitat for the armadillo. In Texas, you'll see armadillo races, armadillos on leashes, armadillos wearing bandannas, armadillos drinking beer and armadillos riding in pickups. Only in Texas.

Hoots 'N Hollers

Featuring "Texas Traffic"

I just love some of the Texas bumper stickers on our cars and trucks. I personally wouldn't have a bumper sticker, but I do admit to quite a few chuckles while reading them on other people's vehicles. Let me give you some examples of the more prevalent ones we see in Texas:

OK! I'm not a native Texan, but I got here as soon as I could!	Luv NY? Take I-35 due north!	Eat more possum
TEXAN by choice	SECEDE	Honk if you love TEXAS
Don't Mess With TEXAS	Drive 90 Freeze a Yankee	I Brake For Armadillos
Welcome, Ya'll Now go home!	On the 8th day God created TEXAS	Naturalized TEXAN
Yankee by birth Texan by choice	GOD BLESS TEXAS	If this truck was a horse, I'd already have shot it!
My kid can beat up your honor student	TEXAS Love it or leave it!	It's hard to be humble when you're from Texas

When I pull up behind a car or truck, I don't give a rat's rump if the occupant loves their spouse, what kind of dog they have, if they're pro-choice, if their kid is an honor student, if they play bingo, what church they attend, what radio station they listen to, where they've traveled, where they dance country, their favorite restaurant, etc., etc., etc. It's boring and it doesn't help the looks of the car or truck either. Having said that, I must reiterate that I do find some bumper stickers funny, and I hope you do too.

Let's talk about "Texas Traffic." Texas has fast and crazy drivers. We have a whole host of drivers who only have one speed. The problem is they go straight, turn and back-up all at that same speed! We have a few "slow pokes." We have more than our share of "Looky Lous." Wherever there is blood and gore on the streets and highways, most Texans want to view it. Most of our feeder streets, or approach ramps, are too short and sharply angled to keep us from entering the freeways gracefully. The ramps look as though they were drawn by drunk engineers, or installed as a cruelty joke. Considering all this, we do pretty well! Most Texans are not courteous drivers by nature. Whenever possible, we will "cut" someone off just for fun. Most Texans think pedestrian lanes are marked off so that we can more easily locate the pedestrian in order to run him down. Hardly anyone stops for a pedestrian in Texas. When you step off a curb you had better pray, scream and run like hell. Everyone in Texas brakes for armadillos, but no one in Texas brakes for a pedestrian. I saw a pregnant woman step off the curb into a pedestrian lane and start to walk across the street. A man screeched to a stop, put his head out the window and screamed, "Hey, lady, you keep that up and you're going to get knocked down too!' Enough said!

Texans are not big horn blowers. If you honk your horn at a Texan, you'd better be telling him his car is on fire, he has a flat, or he just hit a small child because if you don't have a really good reason for blowing your horn at him, you'll probably be wearing your steering wheel as a hula hoop. When you see this bumper sticker, take it seriously.

> **Keep Honking**
> **I'm reloading!**

You'll see some strange vehicles in Texas. I love the pickup convertibles, the Cadillac pickups, the expensive cars with longhorns on the hood, the horns that play "The Eyes of Texas" and I could go on and on. Just trying to decipher Texas license plates is a hoot. Thousands of people drive vehicles painted representative of their college school colors and I must say it usually looks better on the football uniforms. The big, big, big Texas vehicle, the "Texas Cadillac," is the Chevy Suburban. You're nobody if you don't drive a Suburban (if you are a young family in Texas, that is). Sad, but true. Women love the Suburban even more than the men do. Give a Texas woman a Suburban and you won't get her out of it until you buy her a new one. It doesn't matter what their other car is, Lexus or BMW, the Suburban is hers!

If a Texan finds someone parked in a handicapped space who doesn't belong there, there's good news and bad news; the parked culprit will probably get their neck broken, but the good news is that then they will really qualify for handicapped parking!

It rarely snows in most parts of Texas, and Texans cannot drive on ice or snow. We don't get any practice, we have no snow tires, no chains, no road equipment for snow, etc. We all look like we're playing bumper cars from hell. I know it's hard for most people to believe, but if it ices over or snows even slightly, the schools close, the businesses close and everyone gets the day off!

Red lights are a deadly game in Texas. Here are the rules: When your light turns green, for God's sake, sit still and don't attempt to drive through it. This only means that four cars have already run their yellow light and two more, possibly three, will now run their red light before you can go on your green light. Be vigilant. If you miss your turn you could be there all day. If you're a "little slow" you could be there all week! If you don't understand the rules, take a cab. You won't last the first day without a full understanding of Texas traffic rules. You will notice while parked at red lights that women in Texas use red lights to curl their eyelashes, apply lipstick and comb their hair. I don't know why. I don't make the rules. The majority of men, however, use a red light to shove their fingers up their noses. This gets me crazy! Wives, girlfriends and mothers – please provide these men with tissues!

If you do take a cab in Texas, you'll find the cabbies far nicer than in New York City, for example. If NY cabbies talked to our cowboys and Bubbas the way they speak to people in New York City, the cowboys and Bubbas would drag them out of the cab and drop kick their butts into Oklahoma.

Bubbas and cowboys are very possessive of their pickups. I've noticed since I wrote The Bubba Cookbook with Jokes that Bubbas lean toward Chevys, good ole boys drive Fords and cowboys are about equally split between the two.

★

The older Texas ladies drive big ole luxury cars, and the older they get, the bigger the car gets. Young Texas women drive smaller, faster cars when you can get them out of the Suburban!

It is an experience to drive in Texas. If you decide to fly, Texans are mighty proud of their Southwest Airlines. It is rumored that Texans on their way to Heaven have to change planes in Dallas to get there! I heard that! While you're on board or in the airport pick up a copy of "Texas Monthly," a great, upscale, fun and informative Texas magazine.

Texans also love to cruise. There's nothing worse than being stuck on a cruise ship (no matter how large) with a bunch of rowdy Texans. Just leave them to themselves and maybe on your next cruise you'll be lucky enough to travel with the Hell's Angels or some tamer group.

Whether Texans drive, fly or cruise, we aren't gone from home too long. We're like Scarlet O'Hara and her red earth of Tara. We always come home to the Lone Star State and we always will. Ask a Texan if he has a choice of Heaven or hell, which would he choose. Heaven, of course. But given a choice of Heaven or Texas, the odds are he'll choose Texas!

Cowboys and Bubbas (as a rule) Don't Do:

squid

sun dried tomatoes

water chestnuts

petit fours

quiche (real men do, but cowboys and Bubbas still don't!)

crepes

pineapple pizza

steak tar tar

asparagus (or much else green)

curried anything

feta

anchovies

baked potatoes (any other way, O.K.)

chutney

cold soups

couscous

snails

caviar (unless served from a boot)

hot tea

French wine

cucumber sandwiches

liver

cream cheese (any other cheese, O.K.)

prune cake

parsley

stir fry (not to be confused with calf fries)

meatless main dishes

demitasse

soufflés

jellied meats (neither do I)

paté

pasta salad

congealed salads

high tea

watercress

sushi

Cornish hen

beets

celery

crumpets

French roast

Do You Have "Tex Appeal?"

1. Do you know the difference in chili and Chile?
2. Do you know where the original Neiman Marcus is located?
3. Do you brake for armadillos?
4. Have you ever shopped Sheplers?
5. Is beer your largest food expense?
6. Have you ever said, "If it ain't fried, it ain't mine"?
7. What is Big D?
8. Do you know the difference between the Cotton Bowl and the tidy bowl?
9. How do you pronounce R-O-D-E-O?
10. On which side do you mount a horse?
11. Have you memorized the Dairy Queen menu?
12. Who is "Big Tex"?
13. What do you think of when you hear "Blue Bell"?
14. Describe a "Blue Norther."
15. What is Big Bend?
16. Do you like hotter'n hell salsa?
17. Do you know the difference between the yellow rose and Tokyo Rose?

18. Do you believe neck ties are only for hangings?

19. Do you remember not to squat with your spurs on?

20. Is jerky a regular part of your diet?

21. Do you use over 5,000 toothpicks a year?

22. Are you acquainted with a napkin?

23. Have you ever driven anything other than a pickup?

24. Do you know what to do with a calf after you rope it?

25. Would you ever "Mess with Texas"?

26. Is it hard for you to part with your hat for any reason?

27. Have you ever told anyone they're "cuter'n a possum"?

28. Are your food groups "fried and beer"?

29. Can you speak ten words a second with gusts up to 50?

30. Do you have a belt buckle that weights at least 30 pounds?

31. Do you know where every Wal Mart is in a 200 mile radius?

32. Have you been in at least one tornado?

33. Have you ever said "Where's the Beef?"

Bubba says . . .

"Save a chicken. Eat more beef."

Bubba Does Texas

Bubba just cranked up his pickup and traveled Texas. Here's a little of what he saw – well, there's nothing "little" about Texas! This is what he saw – – – –

Dallas

Big D, little a, double l – a – s Dallas!

I grew up hearing Dallas referred to as "Big D" and everyone in Texas understood that. Dallas is the most sophisticated city in Texas. People still "dress" in Dallas. They don't look like they're about to do yard work, or worse, looking as though they just finished yard work! Dallas is known for the elegant Dallas-based Neiman Marcus department store where the movers and shakers shop, shop, shop. Dallas is home to the three time World Champion Dallas Cowboys as well as the Texas Rangers baseball team, the Dallas Stars hockey team and the Dallas Burn Soccer team. Dallas has a rich cultural heritage, offering the Dallas Symphony and the Dallas Museum of Arts. Dallas has an extraordinary offering of museums, fine world-class hotels and restaurants and a fabulous night life. Try the West-End district for a more family-oriented experience or Deep Ellum for a trendy and eclectic night out on the town. The Mansion on Turtle Creek is a must. It's a Texas tradition for the people in the know. Dallas is a great city!

Houston

Houston is the fourth largest city in the U.S. and the largest city in Texas. Houston is a sprawling mass of concrete and freeways, but interspersed with lovely landscaping and friendly neighborhoods. Houston has good shopping, restaurants and hotels, a great city for conventions. Houston is home to the Astrodome, the first of the domed stadiums. The Space Center is nearby. Don't miss the Alley Theater, Worthem Theater Center and Jones Hall, all wonderful facilities. There's the Children's Museum and the Houston Museum of Natural Science and several other museums to visit. The Menil Collection is also available. Houstonians enjoy Astroworld, a large and fun theme park close to the

Astrodome. Historic Galveston Island is about an hour away and worth the trip. The San Jacinto Monument is just minutes away also. You can always find something in Houston to do!

Ft. Worth

Ft. Worth is a city most often associated with the stockyards. Actually, it is a very nice city loaded with Museums and restaurants and is the proud home of Texas Christian University. Visit the Amon Carter Museum as well as the Modern Art Museum and Kimbell Art Museum. Also, visit the Sid Richardson Collection of Western Art. Ft. Worth enjoys the opera and ballet as well. In nearby Arlington there is the long-time fun 6 Flags. Ft. Worth also has a zoo, Good City!

San Antonio

A unique Texas city that could just as easily be a setting in Mexico around every corner. Great home to restaurants, museums, parks, the Riverwalk and the Alamo. The hotels are world class. San Antonio is a fun place to visit even for Texans. Visit the Witte Museum, McNay Art Museum, Institute of Texan Cultures, Museum of Art and Mission Trail. Don't forget Sea World, 6 Flags Fiesta Texas, Brackenridge Park, the Riverwalk and the Alamo. You could easily spend days enjoying San Antonio. I love the Riverwalk and the North Star Mall has always been a real favorite. There are so many good restaurants and hotels for you to enjoy. My favorite? I still like Mi Tierra. I love San Antonio.

Austin

Nestled right up to the "hill country" in central Texas that LBJ made so well known is Austin, a beautiful lush rolling city with Town Lake running through downtown. Downtown has quite a nightlife on historic 6th Street and also the newer downtown area known as "District." Austin is the "Live Music Capital of the World." I consider Austin a "shabby-chic" city where liberals and conservatives meet head on on a daily basis. Visit the LBJ Library on the beautiful University of Texas campus. Learn to say "Hook 'em Horns!" While on campus visit Bass Concert Hall and the Irwin Center, a great facility for all kinds of large events. Austin has lovely old hotels and an abundance of new ones as well. Restaurants are plentiful and good, really good. Visit the Capital building while downtown. It is larger than the Capital building in D.C., being true to Texas style. Austin has beautiful lakes to visit, Lake Travis being the largest. Count down to sunset at the Oasis, a restaurant overlooking Lake Travis and boasting 27 deck levels. The Margaritas are good and the atmosphere fun. Barton Springs is a must to see, a very large spring fed swimming pool in Zilker Park. It's very pretty. Austin has charming old homes and buildings such as Caswell House. The Governor's Mansion is charming. If you like funk and great Mexican food eat at Chuy's. Another really good Texas-Southwest restaurant is Z-Tejas. Sullivan's is a superb restaurant with the best steaks ever. The onion rings are a must. Visit the lovely Arboretum open air mall. Texas Cookie Cutters in the Arboretum has the very best cookies in Texas, in my opinion. Visit the French Legation, Elizabet Ney Museum and the newly refurbished Darrell K. Royal Memorial Stadium. Darrell Royal remains in Austin and still walks on water. Austin has some great Austin-based companies. I can't name them all, but a very few of them are Dell, Whole Foods, Tivoli and National Instruments. We have John Kelso keeping us informed on "Bubba," Cactus Pryor still giving us a chuckle and don't forget Sam & Bob in the morning! I could go on forever about Austin. It's a beautiful city and it's home to me!

El Paso

El Paso is a large city close to New Mexico to the west and bordering Mexico below. The Mexican city across the border is Juarez. El Paso is largely an hispanic population and steeped in Mexican traditions. Visit the El Paso Museum of Art as well as Mission Trail. El Paso is host for the Sun Bowl. Visit H&H Carwash for some fun. The locals eat at Kiki's!

Corpus Christi

Corpus Christi is a sparkling jewel of a city situated on the Gulf of Mexico. Visit Padre Island National Seashore, Aransas National Wildlife Refuge, Texas State Aquarium, Corpus Christi Museum of Science & History and the USS Lexington Museum on the bay. Corpus has good restaurants and hotels. There are lots of beautiful condos to lease on the beach. It's a fun vacation city. You can drive on down the coast to South Padre if you like and even more casual setting popular with the "teen set and spring breakers."

Waco

Waco is home to the Baylor Bears. Baylor has a pretty campus. My daughters both have a degree from Baylor and one of them an undergraduate from S.M.U. in Dallas, so these are two cities I am familiar with. One daughter lives in Waco, the other in Austin. Waco is also home to the Dr. Pepper Museum and the Texas Ranger Hall of Fame. Waco has a real "restaurant row" on Valley Mills Drive. There is just about any food one could wish for!

Bryan-College Station

Sort of in the "middle of nowhere" is Bryan-College Station. The claim to fame there is Aggieland, home to the Texas A&M Aggies. If you formed a triangle with Waco to the north, Austin to the south and College Station to the east, there it is! A&M has the proud distinction of having the George Bush Library. It is worth going there to view that. While there eat at the Dixie Chicken. Does that sound like a Texas restaurant, or what?

Lubbock

Lubbock is the proud home of Texas Tech University. It has the Godbold Culture Center, Mackenzie Park, Lubbock Music Festival and Prairie Dog Town. Also, visit the Buddy Holly Statue and Walk of Fame. Eat at Tom & Bingo's Hickory Pit Bar-B-Q! Also Gordito's. Friendly people!

Amarillo, Abilene & San Angelo

These are three nice small Texas cities. Stop in Amarillo at Dyer's Bar-B-Que or The Stockyard's Café. Try Mr. T's, Zentuer's Steakhouse and Major Grenada while in San Angelo. Also, Henry's Diner and the Pack Saddle in San Angelo. In Abilene it seems that Sharon and Joe Allen have it going for barbecue, fish and catering. It seems that they have several restaurants, and good ones. These are three towns that Texans drive through quite often. I know I do on the way skiing. Now we know where to stop! Just 25 miles southeast of Amarillo and 12 miles east of Canyon is Palo Dura Canyon State Park. The musical "Texas" is performed there in warm months in an open air theater. It portrays early life in Texas. It's worth the trip!

Other Areas of Interest

The Rio Grande Valley encompasses McAllen, Harlingen, Browsville and South Padre Island. The valley produces wonderful and abundant produce. The Ruby Red Grapefruit is an example.

The West Texas Big Bend area encompasses Big Bend National Park and the Davis Mountains. Visit the McDonald Observatory. The Prude Guest Ranch, not far from Ft. Davis, continues to be a wonderful place to do the "Texas things." Great place for kids. The Midland-Odessa area is nearby.

★

The East Texas Piney Woods is a lovely area of Texas. Enjoy the hiking and nature trails, fishing in the many lakes. Visit the National Forest. The Pine trees are plentiful. East Texas is a mecca for lumbermen. Tyler is a lovely city located in east Texas.

The MetroPlex encompasses the Temple-Belton-Killeen area and historic Salado. In Salado visit the Stagecoach Inn. I love that place!

Some things you'll probably never hear Bubba say . . .

Great quiche!

Checkmate.

I just love cats.

Pass the artichokes, please.

Let me get the door.

What wine would you suggest?

Let's do lunch.

Buy whatever you like, dear.

I need a new suit.

Let's start with antipasto.

What time is our bridge game?

Cute poodle.

My stock just went up 3 points.

I think I'll test drive a Lexus.

What time does the opera start?

Look at this great tie.

Let's play tennis.

Champagne all around!

Buy me a Wall Street Journal while you're out.

Let's take dancing lessons.

I think I'll mow the lawn now.

Let's go shopping.

Texts Tidbit

There is no more famous ranch in Texas than the tiny eleven acre ranch known as the "Chicken Ranch" located just outside the LaGrange city limits just 2 blocks from the Houston/Galveston highway. The Chicken Ranch was a Texas brothel with so much business that it is documented as having "mid-level management." The madame moved from Waco to LaGrange about 1905 and set up her house of ill repute inside the city limits by the Colorado river. The town's people tried to close down the "house" causing the madame to relocate her business to the 11 acres known as the "Chicken Ranch" to this day. It operated, very lucratively, until mid 1973. While it was in operation it is rumored that affluent and recognizable customers were regulars; especially those in politics, and including visiting dignitaries. You can easily surmise that more than a little "scratch" changed hands at the Chicken Ranch.

★ *LaGrange is a nice city and a regular stop for traveling people. Visit Prause Meat Market for good Texas barbecue.*

Whore's d'oeuvres

Appetizers from the "Chicken Ranch"

Paprika Port Cheese Balls

1	pound cream cheese	1/4	teaspoon paprika
1	pound finely grated sharp Cheddar cheese	1/4	teaspoon Worcestershire
1/4	pound Bleu cheese		Port wine
1	teaspoon grated onion	1	cup very finely chopped pecans
1/2	teaspoon minced garlic		

Have all cheeses at room temperature. Put all ingredients in mixer along with just enough port wine to soften cheeses. Chill just until you can shape into a ball or a log. Roll in nuts and refrigerate for several days before you use it.

Cactus Jack's Pico de Gallo

4	large chopped tomatoes	1/2	cup chopped cilantro
3/4	cup chopped onion	1/4	cup lime juice
3	jalapeño peppers, seeded and finely chopped		Salt and pepper to taste

Combine all ingredients and refrigerate. Makes about 2-1/2 cups.

Comal County Guacamole

4	avocados	1	teaspoon salt
2	medium tomatoes	1	teaspoon lemon juice
1	clove garlic, minced	1/4	teaspoon pepper
1	small onion		

Cut avocados in half and remove the pit. Peel and mash pulp with a fork until creamy. Add other ingredients and stir well. Chill and serve with chips.

★

Tejas Salsa Verde

4-5	Serrano chiles	2	large cloves garlic, crushed
2	cups chopped fresh tomatillos OR canned tomatillos, drained	1	tablespoon grated white onion
1/3	cup fresh cilantro leaves, chopped,	2	tablespoons fresh lime juice
6	green onions, chopped	1/2	teaspoon salt

Place the serranos on a baking sheet and broil, turning the chiles occasionally, until the skin is dark and blistered. Remove from heat and place the serranos in a plastic bag. Allow them to steam for 20 minutes or so, then remove from bag and peel off the skin. Chop the serranos. Combine serranos and all remaining ingredients and chill, covered, for at least 1 hour.

Salsa will keep, refrigerated, for several days.

Red Hot Texas Sauce

1	(28 oz.) can of tomatoes	1	teaspoon celery seed
5	red bell peppers	1	teaspoon mustard seed
5	green bell peppers	1	tablespoon finely chopped cilantro
10	jalapeños, seeds too		
1	large finely chopped onion	1	tablespoon salt
1	cup vinegar		

Put peppers through the blender. Add tomatoes for a few seconds to the blender. Add all ingredients together and cook for 25 minutes. Seal in sterilized jars. You may refrigerate this when cool or may be processed in a hot water bath. It makes approximately 2 pints.

Great Gifts!

Drunk Chili Con Queso

2 cups grated sharp Cheddar (about 1/4 pound)
2 cups grated Monterey Jack (about 1/4 pound)
2 tablespoons all-purpose flour
1 small onion, minced
1 tablespoon unsalted butter

3/4 cup beer (not dark)
1/2 cup drained canned tomatoes, chopped fine
1 bottle pickled jalapeño chili, minced (wear rubber gloves)
Tortilla chips

In a bowl toss the cheeses with the flour and reserve the mixture. In a large heavy saucepan cook the onion in the butter on medium-low, stirring constantly until it is softened. Add beer, tomatoes, and jalapeño, then simmer the mixture for 5 minutes. Add the reserved cheese mixture by 1/2 cupsful to the beer mixture, stirring after each addition until the cheeses are melted. Serve the dip with the tortilla chips or tortillas.

Padre Green Chili Dip

1 oz. dried New Mexican green chile
1 tablespoon chopped roasted green chile (New Mexican or Poblano)

8 oz. sour cream
2 cloves garlic (minced)
1/2 teaspoon onion salt

Place green chiles in blender and grind until powdered. Combine chili powder with sour cream. Mix in the remaining ingredients. Refrigerate at least one hour. Keeps for 3-4 days.

Bubba says . . .

"We don't give a damn how you did it up north!"

★

Quickie Quesadillas

8   flour tortillas
1/2   lb. mild Cheddar cheese
2-4 fresh jalapeños, thinly sliced
1/2   cup sour cream

1-2 teaspoons ground dried red chile (Ancho or New Mexican
1   cup salsa or pico de gallo

Preheat oven to 350° F. Place four tortillas on baking sheet and top evenly with cheese. Top with jalapeño slices and sprinkle with red chile. Then top with remaining tortillas. Bake 12-15 minutes or until cheese melts and bubbles. Cut into quarters and garnish with salsa and sour cream.

Crab Dip

1   7 oz. can drained crab
1   cup mayonnaise
1/2   cup sour cream
1   tablespoon sherry
2   teaspoons finely chopped parsley

1   teaspoon lemon juice
1/4   teaspoon paprika
1/4   teaspoon Worcestershire
1/4   teaspoon onion salt
1/4   teaspoon garlic salt

Combine all ingredients (making sure there is no shell). Chill well before serving.

Fabulous Fried Onion Rings

1 1/2 cups flour
1   teaspoon baking powder
1 1/2 teaspoons salt
2   eggs, beaten

1   cup milk
1   teaspoon shortening, melted
Onions, peeled and sliced into rings
Vegetable oil

Sift dry ingredients together. Stir in eggs, milk and shortening into flour mixture. Beat until smooth. Dip rings into batter and drop into 375° F. vegetable oil. Fry about 2 minutes or until golden brown.

★

Pickled Jalapeños
Whoa!

4	cups vinegar	1	tablespoon + 1 teaspoon
1	cup olive oil		pickling spices
1	tablespoon + 1 teaspoon salt		

Heat mixture to a boil and pour over washed jalapeño peppers that have been patted dry and packed tightly into quart jars (2). Cover well and leave one inch space at the top. Seal jars and process 10 minutes in a hot water bath.

★ I like to put thin rounds of onion in the jars as well.

Stuffed Mushroom Caps

12	medium to small-sized mushrooms		Italian-flavored bread crumbs
			Salt and pepper to taste
1/4	cup freshly chopped onion	1/2	teaspoon paprika
1/4	stick of margarine or butter	1	teaspoon sage
1	clove garlic	1	fried bacon slice
1/4	cup of white wine		

Remove stems from caps and chop into fine pieces. Chop 1/4 cup onions and 1 section of garlic and saute in 1/4 stick of melted butter in frying pan. Add chopped mushroom stems and saute until stems are soft. Flavor with salt, pepper, paprika, and sage to taste. Add wine and heat a couple of minutes. Crumble in 1 slice of fried bacon. Add Italian-flavored bread crumbs until mixture is stiff enough to spoon. Coat inside of caps with soft butter, gently spoon mixture into caps, and broil stuffed caps under broiler for 3-4 minutes.

Bubba says . . .

"Texas, love it or leave it!"

Hot Chicken Bites

1	cup minced cooked chicken	1	tablespoon curry powder
1¼	cup dried bread crumbs, divided	1	tablespoon grated onion
2	tablespoons minced parsley	1	egg, well beaten
¼	cup mayonnaise	¼	teaspoon salt

Mix chicken, 2 tablespoons bread crumbs, curry, parsley, onion and mayonnaise to form small balls. Roll each in beaten egg, then in bread crumbs. Repeat. Bake 450° F. about 12 minutes. Serve with a sauce made of 1/2 honey mustard and 1/2 mayonnaise of choice.

Laredo Artichoke Dip

1	6 oz. jar artichoke hearts, drained and finely chopped	2	teaspoons grated onion
1	cup mayonnaise	1	teaspoon minced garlic
½	cup freshly grated Parmesan cheese	½	cup grated Cheddar cheese
		¼	teaspoon pepper
		¼	teaspoon salt

Combine all ingredients and mix well. Pour into a buttered 1 qt. baking dish and bake 375° F. about 20 minutes.

Bubba says . . .

"Only fools and newcomers predict Texas weather."

Easy Ham & Cheese Pinwheels

1	small package flour tortillas	1	tablespoon honey
2	8 oz. packages cream cheese	1	tablespoon dried parsley
12	large deli slices of ham	1	tablespoon well drained, finely
2	teaspoons grated onion		chopped pimento
2	tablespoons mayonnaise	$1/4$	teaspoon cayenne
1	teaspoon mustard		

Use room temperature cream cheese. Place all ingredients except tortillas and ham in mixer. Mix until well blended. Lay tortillas out on waxed paper and equally spread the mixture on them. Put ham slices on each tortillas. Roll tortillas and place in the refrigerator after placing them on a cookie sheet and wrapping them with plastic wrap. After 2 hours take out and slice into 1/3" rounds. Place a layer of these on cookie sheet and top with waxed paper. Repeat until all rollups are used. When you serve them you can serve as is or put a toothpick through each pinwheel if desired.

Very Texas Jalapeño Jelly

$3/4$	cup chopped jalapeño peppers	$1 1/3$	cup vinegar
$3/4$	cup chopped bell peppers	$1/2$	cup water
$5 1/4$	cup sugar	1 bottle Certo	

Place peppers, sugar, vinegar and water in a large pot. Boil 5 minutes. Remove from heat and let cool 20 minutes. Add Certo, mix well and return to burner. Bring jelly to a full boil then remove from heat. Stir well and pour into jelly glasses. Seal with paraffin after jelly has completely cooled. This makes a half dozen jars.

For holiday presents use half red and half green bell peppers for pretty gifts. Also, try serving this with crackers and cream cheese as an appetizer sometime. Men like the taste.

★

Beef Jerky

1 flank steak cut with grain into thin strips. Cover steak with soy sauce and marinate overnight. Add 1 teaspoon liquid smoke and marinate overnight again. Put meat on a cooling rack and season with 2 teaspoons lemon pepper, 2 teaspoons salt, and 2 teaspoons garlic powder. Place rack in 150° F. oven for about 14 hours.

Sweet and Sour Meatballs

1	pound lean ground beef	1	can (20 ounces) pineapple chunks, drained and juice reserved
1	egg		
1/2	cup seasoned bread crumbs		
1	tablespoon dried onion flakes	1/4	cup plus 2 tablespoons water
1	tablespoon green pepper, chopped	3	tablespoons rice wine vinegar
2	tablespoons teriyaki sauce	1	tablespoon soy sauce
	Non-stick vegetable cooking spray	1	large green pepper, cut into 1/2-inch cubes
3	tablespoons cornstarch		
1/2	cup brown sugar, lightly packed		

Preheat oven to 400° F. In medium bowl combine ground beef, egg, bread crumbs, onion flakes, green pepper and teriyaki sauce. Shape 30 meatballs (about 1 tablespoon beef mixture per meatball). Coat 10 x 15 x 1-inch baking pan with non-stick spray. Arrange meatballs on pan and bake 15-20 minutes or until meatballs are no longer pink in center. Meanwhile, in 2-quart microwave-safe dish, combine cornstarch and brown sugar. Stir in green pepper then microwave on high for 3 minutes, stirring halfway through. Fold in meatballs and pineapple chunks. Microwave at High for 2 minutes or until mixture is heated throughout.

Succulent Short Ribs

1	side of baby back pork ribs	1	teaspoon vinegar
2	onions, quartered	1	teaspoon mustard
2	cloves crushed garlic	2	tablespoons brown sugar
1/4	cup ketchup	2	tablespoons pineapple juice
1	tablespoon soy sauce	1/4	teaspoon salt
2	tablespoons honey	1/4	teaspoon pepper
2	tablespoons chili sauce	1	teaspoon margarine

Fill a roaster with 1-2" of boiling water. Add ribs and onion to water, cover, bake 1 hour in a preheated 325° F. oven. Remove ribs and onion to drain in paper towels. Pat dry. Pour out water and dry pan. Add ribs and onion back to pan with all other ingredients that have been combined and stirred into a mix. Pour mix over ribs. Bake 1-1/2 to 2 hours at 300° F. turning once and basting several times during this baking. Remove lid, turn oven to 375° F. and brown for about 20 minutes turning once. After removing ribs to a platter, pour the leftover sauce into a gravy boat and serve it also.

Serves 4.

Crab Canapes

1	jar (5 oz.) Old English cheese spread	1/2	teaspoon onion salt
		1/4	teaspoon paprika
1	stick margarine	1	7 oz. can drained crabmeat
1	teaspoon mayonnaise	8	split English muffins
1/2	teaspoon garlic salt		

Mix margarine, cheese, mayonnaise, garlic salt, onion salt and crabmeat together. Spread on muffins. (You can freeze them at this point for later if you wish)You can use them this size for a luncheon entree or cut them into about 6 pieces for canapes.

Just before serving broil light brown. If frozen, thaw first.

★

Crabmeat Stuffed Mushrooms

30	large mushrooms	1	well beaten egg
1	onion, finely chopped	1/2	cup grated Cheddar cheese
1/2	cup fine bread crumbs	1	tablespoon butter
1/2	cup crabmeat	1/4	teaspoon garlic salt
2	teaspoons Worcestershire		

Wash mushrooms, dry. Remove stems and chop with onion. Over a low heat sauté all ingredients except mushroom caps and cheese.

Fill mushroom caps with filling. Place in a baking dish and sprinkle with Cheddar cheese. Bake 350° F. 18 minutes.

★   I sprinkle with parmesean although it isn't called for in my recipe.

★ *Davy Crockett, upon his defeat for re-election, told the Tennessee Legislature, "You go to hell. I'm going to Texas."*

Texas Tidbit

You just never drive up to a Texas country club, elite private club or posh restaurant and see a sign reading "No shirt, no shoes, no service." No joke! However, possibly in the same block there will be a sign stating this at a club or restaurant with a different clientele. These signs are prevalent all over Texas. The "white collar" diner is well acquainted with the social graces and usually practices them. Texas has an abundance of socialites. The "blue collar" group usually wears a shirt to a restaurant. What else would they wipe their mouths on? This group has what we refer to as Blue Collar Country Clubs. There are juke joints, or beer joints, where Bubba and cowboys alike feel comfortable. The attire is jeans and tee shirt or western shirt, boots, caps and stetsons. Music is blaring country & western and the dance is Texas Swing, Texas Two Step, Cotton-eyed Joe, line dancing and the like. They can yell obscenities and be "very relaxed." You won't catch Bubba at the opera or even the symphony, but oddly enough you will find the "white collars" at the joints. The white collars and the blue collars also come together on a regular basis at the medium priced Texas restaurants featuring such Texas staples as chicken fried steak, burgers, catfish and barbecue. It seems that not everyone in Texas knows good manners, but most Texans know good food! There seems to be a different set of rules for these two groups. If a socialite is inebriated he is quietly refused another drink and a cab is discreetly called. If a Bubba or cowboy gets drunk in a joint he is tossed out on his ear only after a ruckus has taken place. These are the rules! Bubbas and cowboys don't like to remove their hats or caps and don't wear ties. This precludes them from even entering a critically acclaimed establishment. The white collars are dressed for the joint in "whatever." I do suspect if a tie was worn they would duly hang him with it! We have lots of joints in Texas, some high class and others low class. Everyone in all the joints seems happy. I don't understand how – the music is all about divorce, getting drunk, mama, prison, jails, and being generally lovesick. It's hard to be cheered up by all this! Oh, well – it's Texas!

★

Slurps & Burps

Soups and Salads

Cowboy Soup

2	lbs. ground chuck	3	diced potatoes
2	chopped onions	1	cup macaroni
2	chopped bell peppers	1	can ranch style beans
3	cloves garlic, minced	1	15 oz. can of water
2	15 oz. cans diced tomato	1/2	teaspoon chili powder
1	can whole kernel corn		Salt and pepper to taste

Saute meat, onion, peppers and garlic. Drain. Dump everything in pot but the potatoes and macaroni. Simmer an hour. Add potatoes and macaroni and simmer, stirring several times, about 30 minutes.

Feeds 6 hungry cowboys!

Yucky Green Stuff
(Split Pea Soup)

8	cups water	1	teaspoon salt
1	lb. dried split peas	1/4	teaspoon pepper
1	lb. smoked ham, boneless	2	carrots, chopped
1	medium onion, chopped	2	stalks celery, chopped

Heat water and peas to boiling then boil for 2 minutes and remove from heat. Cover and let sit for 1 hour. Add ham (whole), onion, salt and pepper, then cover and simmer about one hour or until peas are tender. Remove ham and cut into bite-sized pieces. Stir ham, carrots, and celery into soup. Cover and simmer about 45 minutes or until veggies are tender.

Serves 3-5

Cowboys say . . .

"Bury me with my boots on and don't forget my hat."

French Onion Soup

1¹/₂ lbs. red onions, peeled and halved	¹/₂ teaspoon Worcestershire sauce
¹/₃ cup margarine or butter	¹/₂ teaspoon salt
3 cubes beef flavored bouillon	¹/₂ teaspoon black pepper
4 cups water	4 ounces Swiss Cheese
¹/₂ cup dry white wine	¹/₄ loaf French bread

Slice onions, thinly. Melt butter in 2-quart Dutch oven. Slowly cook onions in butter about one minutes or until lightly browned. Stir in Worcestershire sauce, salt and pepper. Shred cheese.To serve soup, place a thin slice of French bread into the bottom of each individual ovenware serving bowl. Ladle soup into bowls. Top with a thick layer of shredded cheese. Place under broiler or microwave until cheese melts.

Serve immediately – serves 4.

Beer Broccoli Cheese Soup

1 cup diced onions	1 bunch broccoli
1 cup diced celery	1 can beer
1 cup diced carrots	2-inch Velveeta cheese, chunked
1 cup diced mushrooms	6 oz. Cheddar cheese, grated
³/₄ cup butter	2 tablespoons grated parmesan cheese
¹/₂ cup flour	
1 teaspoon dry mustard	Salt and pepper to taste
5 cups chicken stock	

Sauté the diced vegetables in butter. Mix flour and mustard into sautéed vegetables and add the chicken stock to mixture. Cook five minutes. Cut broccoli into bite-sized pieces, then steam until tender-crisp. Add broccoli, beer and cheeses to soup and simmer 10-15 minutes. Salt and pepper to taste.

★

Southwest Cheese Soup

1	small can whole kernel corn	3/4	teaspoon cumin
1/4	cup corn oil	2	cups chicken stock
2	garlic cloves, minced	1/2	cup uncooked rice
1	cup chopped onion	1	cup milk
1	poblano pepper, seeded and diced	2	cups heavy cream
1	jalapeño pepper, seeded and diced	4	oz. American cheese, shredded
1	red bell pepper, seeded and diced	4	oz. Monterrey Jack cheese, shredded
1/4	cup flour		Salt and cayenne pepper to taste

Sauté onion, garlic and peppers in oil until tender. Stir in flour and cook for about 15 minutes. Add cumin. Slowly add chicken stock, stirring well. Add rice and simmer for 15 to 20 minutes. Add milk and cream and heat through. Add cheeses at the last minute and do not boil after that. Natural cheeses will curdle if boiled. Processed cheeses will not curdle, but the flavor is not as intense. If soup is too thick, thin with additional milk or stock.

Sausage Bean Chowder

1	lb. pork sausage links	1	large or 2 smaller potatoes, diced
2	16 oz. cans kidney beans	1	bay leaf
1	20 oz. can tomatoes, chopped	2	teaspoons garlic salt
4	cups water	1/2	teaspoon pepper (cracked)
2	onions, chopped	1/2	teaspoon thyme
1	green pepper, chopped		

Bake the links in foil at 375° for 30 minutes, then cut into bite-sized pieces. Don't get burned by grease when cutting.

In large Dutch oven combine all ingredients except potatoes. Cover and slowly simmer 1 hour. Add the potatoes, stir. Check salt and pepper level and adjust at this time. Remove bay leaf, cover, and simmer until potatoes are done (not mushy, but done).

Serves 6-8.

Next Damned Day
Chicken Noodle Soup

4	lb. hen	4	chicken bouillon cubes
8	cups water	1/4	teaspoon nutmeg
1	large onion, chopped	1/2	teaspoon small cracked
3	carrots, chopped		pepper
3	ribs celery, chopped	2	tablespoons dried parsley
1/2	cup frozen peas	6	ounces egg noodles

The day before you serve this soup, place all ingredients except noodles in a large stock pot. Simmer the chicken slowly for 1 hour. Remove chicken to cool. Make bite-sized pieces of chicken and place them in a freezer bag in the refrigerator until tomorrow. When stock pot is cool place it in the refrigerator also. The next day remove stock pot from the refrigerator. The fat will be congealed on the top of the soup. Remove it and bring the soup to a boil. Place the chicken in the pot and boil 10 minutes. Put the noodles in the pot and boil until tender.

Serves a large family.

Bubba says . . .
"Texans trade in their Cadillacs when the ashtrays are full."

Shrimp Gumbo

2   cups onion, chopped
1   tablespoon garlic, minced
$1^1/_2$ cups celery, chopped
$^1/_2$ cup bell pepper, chopped
3   lbs. shelled & deveined shrimp
$^1/_2$ lb. fresh, sliced okra
About 3 bay leaves
$4^1/_2$ quarts cold water
$1^1/_2$ cups flour
$^1/_2$ cups bacon dripping
$^1/_2$ cup Crisco

3   peeled, shopped ripe tomatoes
    OR
1   large can tomatoes, chopped
2   teaspoons salt
$^1/_2$ teaspoons pepper
Tabasco to taste
1   small can tomato sauce (if desired, some people like more of a tomato flavor, some less)

Make a roux with Crisco, drippings and flour over low heat, stirring constantly. Add water slowly. Add onion, garlic while adding water. Then over a higher heat, add celery and bell pepper. Add bay leaves, okra and tomatoes. Cook down over lowered heat. Add shrimp, continue simmering for 20 minutes. Stir often.

Serve over rice. Serves a happy crowd!

Gulf Seafood Soup

1   oz. butter
4   onions, chopped
6   ounces prawns
8   ounces crabmeat, flaked
2   tablespoons flour
$1^1/_2$ pints milk
$^1/_2$ teaspoon black pepper

$^1/_4$ teaspoon dry chervil
$^1/_8$ teaspoon cayenne pepper
5   fluid ounces cream
$1^1/_2$ tablespoons whiskey or brandy
2   teaspoons fresh parsley

Melt butter and sauté onions until soft. Add crab, then cook for 1 minute. Stir in flour, add milk, and stir until thick. Lower the heat, add chervil and both peppers. Simmer 10 minutes. Add cream and whiskey and simmer for a few minutes.

Waldorf Salad

4	apples, diced	1/2	cup cool whip
4	ribs celery, chopped	1	teaspoon lemon juice
1/2	cup pecans, chopped	1/4	teaspoon celery seed
1/2	cup mayonnaise		

Toss the apples, celery and pecans in a salad bowl. Gently whisk the mayonnaise, cool whip, lemon juice and celery seed together. Pour over the apples and toss until well coated. Chill until served.

Serves 4-6 people.

Curried Chicken Salad

4	cups cooked chicken, diced	1	tablespoon soy sauce
1 1/2	cups celery, diced	1 1/2	teaspoon curry powder
1	8 oz. can Pineapple Tidbits	1/2	teaspoon cracked pepper
1	8 oz. can water chestnuts, diced	1/2	teaspoon salt
1/2	cup almonds, slivered	4	hard boiled eggs, cut in wedges
2	cups mayonnaise		
1/2	cup sour cream	1	teaspoon dried parsley

Combine all salad ingredients and mix well. Garnish and chill.

Serves 6-8.

Black-Eyed Pea Salad

1	10 oz. package frozen black-eyed peas	1	Tablespoon chopped fresh jalapeño pepper
1/4	cup chopped sweet red pepper	2	tablespoons chopped parsley
1/4	cup chopped green bell pepper	1/4	cup Italian dressing
1/4	cup chopped red onion		

Rinse and drain thawed peas. Mix with other ingredients.

★

Texas Taco Salad

1	lb. ground beef	1/2	head lettuce, shredded
1/4	cup finely chopped green onion	1	tomato, diced
1/4	teaspoon chili powder	1	4 oz can diced olives
1/4	teaspoon black pepper	1	15 oz. can red kidney beans
	Dash salt	1	large bag nacho cheese flavor Dorito chips or Fritos
3/4	cup grated Cheddar cheese	1/4	cup dressing of choice

Brown ground beef in skillet with onion and spices, then drain fat. Combine grated cheese, lettuce, tomato, olives, and beans in large salad bowl. Crumble chips into bite-sized pieces. Just before serving, add beef, Doritos, and dressing to salad and toss.

Chicken Fajita Salad

4	boneless, skinless chicken breast halves	1/2	cup diced bell pepper
1	15 oz. can pinto or black beans, undrained	1/4	cup each chopped green onion, red onion and cilantro,
1	141/2 oz. can cut tomatoes, well drained		Mesquite flavored marinade
4	cups shredded lettuce		Red wine vinegar dressing
			Salsa

Brush chicken with Mesquite Cooking Sauce. Broil or grill 3-5 minutes per side or until done. Baste with mesquite sauce periodically. Slice chicken into thin strips. Combine remaining ingredients with chicken strips and toss with 2 tablespoons salsa and 2 tablespoons dressing. Garnish with guacamole and sour cream, if desired.

Whipped Cream Fruit Salad

1	apple, diced	1	can pineapple chunks, drain and reserve juice
2	bananas, sliced into rounds		
1	large can fruit cocktail, drained	1/2	cup pecans, finely chopped
1	cup cherries, halved	1	small carton Cool Whip
1	orange, peeled and diced	1	cup miniature marshmallows

Fold all ingredients together. If needed, add pineapple juice for the right consistency. Chill until served. If not serving within 2 hours, put the bananas in just before serving.

Refreshing Tomato & Potato Salad

6	small red potatoes	5	teaspoons balsamic vinegar
1/4	cup plus 2 teaspoons extra-virgin olive oil	1	tablespoon minced fresh basil or 1 teaspoon dried, crumbled
1	medium onion, chopped		
1	large garlic clove, minced	1/4	teaspoon dried oregano, crumbled
2	large tomatoes, diced		

Cook potatoes in large pot of boiling salted water until just tender. Drain and cool slightly, then cut potatoes into small pieces and place in large bowl. Next, heat 2 teaspoons olive oil in heavy medium skillet on medium. Add onion and sauté 5 minutes or until translucent. Add garlic and cook 1 minute longer then add onion mixture to potatoes. Add remaining 1/4 cup oil, tomatoes, vinegar, basil and oregano. Toss well and season with salt and pepper to taste.

Serves 3-4.

Bubba says . . .

"Don't squat with your spurs on!"

Black Bean & Corn Salad

2	handsful of black beans, cleaned, soaked and cooked for 8 hours		1	red bell pepper
			5	cloves garlic, minced
1	bag frozen corn		1/4	cup fresh cilantro
1	medium onion		1/4	teaspoon salt
				Juice of one lemon, and one lime

Preheat oven to 350° F. Roast pepper and garlic in oven for about 30 minutes. Roast bell pepper then peel it when it is done. Mix drained beans, cooked corn, chopped onion, cut up pepper, garlic, and cilantro. Add salt to taste, and the juices.

Let sit overnight.

Spicy Mexican Bean Salad

1	red onion, sliced		1	15 oz. can red kidney beans, drained and rinsed
1/4	cup water			
1	tablespoon chili powder		1	15 oz. can white beans, drained and rinsed
1	teaspoon garlic powder			
2	cups cooked green beans		1 1/2	cups frozen corn kernels, thawed
1	15 oz. can black beans, drained and rinsed		2	tablespoons cilantro or parsley

Place the onion in a saucepan with the water and cook about 4-5 minutes or until the onion is soft and separated into rings. Add the chili powder and garlic then stir until well mixed. Remove from heat. Combine all of the ingredients in a large bowl and toss well. Cover and chill for 1 to 2 hours.

★

Creamy Pasta Salad

3   cups DRY corkscrew pasta
1   cup mayonnaise
2   tablespoons lemon juice
2   tablespoons Dijon mustard

1   teaspoon pepper
2¹/₂   cups sliced pepperoni (optional)
1¹/₂   cups seasoned croutons

Cook pasta and drain. In small bowl mix mayonnaise, lemon juice, mustard and pepper. In large bowl, toss pasta, pepperoni and dressing until evenly coated. Toss pasta mixture with 1 cup of croutons just before serving, then top with remaining croutons.

Serves 3-4.

Creamy Coleslaw

1   head cabbage, shredded
1   bell pepper, finely chopped
1   onion, finely chopped
2   carrots, grated
1   cup mayonnaise
¹/₄   teaspoon small cracked pepper

1   tablespoon vinegar or lemon juice
2   teaspoons sugar
1   teaspoon dry mustard
¹/₂   teaspoon salt

Just put all ingredients in a large bowl and mix well. Refrigerate

Gulf Coast Seafood Salad

1	cup mayonnaise	1½	lbs. lump crabmeat
1	cup sour cream	1½	cups frozen green peas
3	tablespoons lemon juice	4	stalks celery, chopped
¼	teaspoons paprika	1	cup fresh grapes, green or red
¼	teaspoon onion salt	1	large Delicious apple,
¼	teaspoon garlic salt		chopped
½	teaspoon small cracked pepper	7	cups salad greens, mixed
4	hard boiled eggs, sliced		lettuce and spinach
1½	lbs. cooked shrimp, cut in two	1	cup parsley

Combine mayonnaise, sour cream, lemon juice, paprika, onion and garlic salts, and cracked pepper and mix well. Refrigerate dressing. Combine rest of the ingredients (except salad greens and eggs) and toss. Place crisp salad greens on salad plates and put salad mixture on the greens. Put the dressing over salad. Garnish with the egg slices and parsley.

Serves about 8-10 hungry people.

Strawberry Spinach Salad

1	large bunch spinach	1	teaspoon dry mustard
10	large strawberries	⅓	cup whine wine
½	cup sugar	⅓	cup vegetable oil
1	teaspoon salt	1	heaping tablespoon poppy seeds

Wash, drain and tear spinach into bite-sized pieces. Place in salad bowl and chill. Slice strawberries and set aside. Mix dressing ingredients (except poppy seeds) together in blender. Stir in poppy seeds. Just before serving, mix dressing with spinach and reserved strawberries.

Overnight Coleslaw

1	head cabbage, shredded	1	carrot, chopped finely
1	bell pepper, chopped finely	1	cup sugar
2	onions, chopped finely		

In large bowl mix ingredients and sprinkle the cup of sugar on top.

Bring to a boil:

2	tablespoons sugar	1	teaspoon dry mustard
1	cup vinegar	1	tablespoon salt
3/4	cup oil	1	teaspoon celery seed

Pour hot mixture over salad. Do not stir. Refrigerate. Stir the next day before serving.

Serves 6-8

Southwest Caesar Dressing

1	cup mayonnaise	1/2	teaspoon Cayenne pepper
1	teaspoon brown sugar	2	tablespoon grated Parmesan cheese
2	tablespoon soy sauce		
3	tablespoons lemon juice		

Salt and pepper to taste

In a small bowl, mix mayonnaise, brown sugar, soy sauce, lemon juice, cayenne pepper and cheese. Blend all ingredients well, then add salt and pepper to taste.

★ *In October, 1930 C. M. (Dad) Joiner discovered the famous East Texas oil field. It's first year it brought in over 100 million barrels of oil and finally covered over 200 square miles.*

Mediterranean Eggplant Salad

1	eggplant		1	teaspoon sugar
2	tomatoes		2	cloves garlic, minced
1	small red onion		2	teaspoons lemon juice
1/4	olive oil		Salt and pepper to taste	
2	teaspoons dried parsley		1/2	cup crumbled Feta cheese
1/3	cup vinegar			

Peel eggplant and cut into slices and place on paper towels. Sprinkle liberally with salt on both sides and leave for 1 hour. Wash salt off and boil slowly for 10 minutes. Drain. Place eggplant on salad plates equally. Put 2 thin layers of onion slices on eggplant. On top of the onion place 2 thin slices of tomato. Crumble feta on top of this.

Whisk the rest of the ingredients together and pour evenly and slowly over the salads, lifting layers to cover all. Serve cold on bed of lettuce. Garnish with black olives.

Italian Vinaigrette Dressing

1/4	cup olive oil		1/2	teaspoon oregano
1/4	cup water		1/2	teaspoon paprika
1/3	cup white vinegar		1/4	teaspoon dry mustard
1	tablespoon granulated sugar		1/8	teaspoon black pepper
2	tablespoons parmesan cheese		1	clove garlic, crushed

Combine oil, water, vinegar, sugar, parmesan cheese, oregano, paprika, mustard, black pepper, and garlic and mix well. Store in the refrigerator up to 2 weeks.

Bubba says . . .

"Born a Texan, live a Texan, die a Texan!"

Buttermilk Dressing

Cowboys and Bubbas' favorite! Try a couple of minced jalapeños in this for those who like spicy Texas dressing.

1	cup mayonnaise	1/2	teaspoon dried dill
1/2	cup buttermilk	1/4	teaspoon garlic powder
2	tablespoons grated parmesan cheese	1/4	teaspoon onion powder
		1/8	pepper
1/2	teaspoon parsley flakes	1	tablespoon milk

Mix together mayonnaise and buttermilk, then stir in cheese, herbs, garlic powder, onion powder, and pepper. Cover and store in refrigerator up to 2 weeks. Add milk as needed to reach desired consistency.

Poppy Seed Dressing

1/2	cup sugar	1/3	cup cider vinegar
1	teaspoon salt	1	tablespoon lemon juice
1	teaspoon dry mustard	1	cup salad oil
1/2	teaspoon onion powder	1 1/2	tablespoon poppy seeds

Combine sugar, salt, dry mustard, onion powder, cider vinegar and lemon juice and stir until sugar dissolves. Add oil in increments and beat well as dressing thickens. Add the oil very slowly in a thin, thin, stream! Stir in poppy seeds. Store in refrigerator and shake well before serving. Best served over fresh fruit salad. Oddly enough, men like this dressing.

Bubba says . . .
"A good dog is hard to keep on the porch!"

Texas Tidbit

The Yellow Rose of Texas

Emily Morgan, a young mulatto girl and probably a slave, was the Texas "Honey" given the name "The Yellow Rose of Texas," or so the Texas legend goes. It is rumored that Santa Anna, leader of the Mexican army, was so besotted by the pretty girl that he let his guard down while Sam Houston mustered his "rag tag" troops against him after the siege at the Alamo. The battle took only 16 minutes and Sam Houston and his men had soundly defeated Santa Anna at San Jacinto. Whether Emily Morgan is responsible for the defeat or not it was a proud day in Texas history and whether Santa Anna was caught with his guard down or his pants down – God Bless Texas!

★ *Visit the San Jacinto Monument and battlefield at San Jacinto near Houston when in the area. Be sure to dine at the San Jacinto Inn for some distinctive food.*

Speaking of roses – Tyler, Texas is the rose capitol of the world. It was the home of Earl Campbell, the University of Texas' Heisman Trophy running back and known by football fans everywhere as "The Tyler Rose." Earl makes his home in Austin and makes some mighty fine sausage. Look for his label; it's everywhere.

Bread, Butter & "Honey"

Better known as the "Yellow Rose of Texas"

GIVE US THIS DAY

San Jacinto Inn Biscuits

Where Santa Anna was defeated in only minutes after being slowed down at the Alamo enough for our troops to rally to defeat him; led by Sam Houston.

4	cups flour	1	teaspoon sugar
3	teaspoons baking powder	3/4	cups shortening
1	teaspoon salt	1 3/4	cups milk

Sift flour and dry ingredients together in a large mixing bowl. Add shortening and milk and work dough with hands on a lightly floured surface. Roll out dough and cut with biscuit cutter. Bake 400° F. 10-15 minutes or until lightly browned.

20 large biscuits.

Texas Beer Biscuits

2	cups unbleached flour	1/4	cups shortening
3	teaspoons baking powder	3/4	cups beer
1	teaspoon salt		

Preheat oven to 450° F. Sift dry ingredients together. Cut in shortening until it has cornmeal consistency. Stir in beer, kneed lightly, then roll out to 1/2-inch thickness. Bake 10-12 minutes or until golden brown.

Makes 12 to 15 biscuits.

Bubba says . . .

"No dancin' on tables with your spurs on!"

Little Cheddar Biscuits

2	cups unbleached flour		1	cup butter, room temperature
1	teaspoon dry mustard		10	oz. sharp cheddar, grated
1	teaspoon paprika		1	teaspoon Worcestershire
1/4	teaspoon baking powder			sauce

Combine the flour, dry mustard, paprika and baking powder in a medium bowl. Beat the butter at medium speed until light and fluffy. Slowly beat in the cheddar cheese and Worcestershire sauce. Gradually add the flour mixture, stirring with a fork until well blended. On a lightly flowered surface, shape the dough into a long roll about 1-3/4-inches in diameter. Wrap in plastic wrap or foil, place on a platter and refrigerate for at least 2 hours, preferably overnight. Preheat the oven to 325° F. Slice the dough about 1/3 inch thick then roll each slice into a ball. Flatten slightly and place on an ungreased baking sheet about 2 inches apart. Bake 8 minutes or until slightly brown on the bottom.

East Texas Sweet Potato Biscuits

8	oz. cooked sweet potato, chilled		1/2	teaspoon salt
1/3	oz. buttermilk, chilled		1/4	teaspoon baking soda
1	cup soft wheat flour		3	tablespoons vegetable
1 1/2	teaspoon baking powder			shortening
1	teaspoon sugar		1	teaspoon vanilla

Preheat oven to 450° F. and grease baking sheet. Purée sweet potato, vanilla and buttermilk together in blender. Sift dry ingredients into bowl. Use large fork to cut shortening until coarse. Use spatula to fold in sweet potato purée and vanilla then blend with dry ingredients. Flour work space and gently knead dough about 6 turns. Pat out dough and cut with biscuit cutter dipped in flour. Place biscuits on cookie sheet and bake 12-14 minutes or until edges are slightly browned. Rotate cookie sheets if using more than one so biscuits brown evenly.

Firey Jalapeño Hushpuppies

2	cups yellow cornmeal	1	cup buttermilk
1	tablespoon flour	1	egg
1	teaspoon baking powder	2	tablespoons finely chopped onion
1	teaspoon baking soda		
2	teaspoons salt	1/3	cups chopped jalapeño peppers

Combine all ingredients and mix well. Drop by tablespoons into hot grease!

Makes 2-1/4 dozen.

Basic Country Cornbread

1 1/4	cup yellow cornmeal	1	teaspoon salt
1	cup flour	2	beaten eggs
1/3	cup sugar	1	cup milk
4	teaspoons baking power	1/4	cup oil

Mix dry ingredients in a bowl. Add wet ingredients and stir, but don't beat. Put into a well greased pyrex dish or greased muffin cups and bake at 400° F. Take out when lightly browned.

★ *Tortillas are the number one selling ethnic bread in America. Texas does it's share toward it's sales.*

★

Jalapeño Cornbread

1¹/4	cup yellow cornmeal		1	teaspoon salt
1	cup flour		2	beaten eggs
2	tablespoons sugar		1	cup milk
4	teaspoons baking powder		1/4	cup oil

Mix dry ingredients in a bowl. Add wet ingredients and stir, but don't beat.

Add:

1	small can while kernel corn, drained		2	tablespoons chopped and drained pimento (optional)
1/2	cup finely chopped onion		1	cup grated cheddar cheese
4	finely chopped & seeded jalapeños			

Stir and pour into a well greased pyrex dish or greased muffin cups and bake at 400° F. Take out when lightly browned.

Luscious Lemon-Poppy Seed Muffins

1/4	cup vegetable oil		2	cups biscuit mix
1	cup milk		1/4	cups poppy seeds
2	eggs		1/4	teaspoon grated lemon peel
1	package lemon instant pudding and pie mix (4-serving pkg.)			

GLAZE

2/3	cup powdered sugar	3¹/2	teaspoon lemon juice

Preheat oven to 375° F. Grease bottom and sides of 12 medium muffin cups or line with paper baking cups. Mix oil, milk, eggs and pudding and pie filling with fork until well blended. Stir in baking mix, poppy seeds and lemon peel and blend thoroughly. Place batter evenly in cups, then bake 25-30 minutes or until light golden brown. Cool 10 minutes; then drizzle with glaze.

To prepare glaze, mix powdered sugar and 3-4 teaspoons lemon juice until mixture is smooth and drizzle over cooled muffins.

★

Spicy Apple Muffins

1 1/2	cups unbleached flour	1/2	cup raisins
3	tablespoons rolled oats	2	small apples, pared/cored/cubed
1	tablespoon baking powder		
1	teaspoons cinnamon	3/4	cup milk, room temp.
1/4	cup applesauce, room temp.	1/2	teaspoons cloves
1/2	cup brown sugar, packed	1	egg white, whipped
1/2	teaspoons nutmeg	1	teaspoon vanilla
1/4	teaspoons salt		

Preheat oven to 350° F. Prepare 12 muffin pans with cooking spray and flour. In a mixing bowl, combine flour, oats, baking powder, cinnamon, nutmeg, cloves, salt and raisins. In another mixing bowl, combine apples, milk, brown sugar, applesauce, and egg white. Mix wet ingredients with dry ingredients just until moistened. Stir in vanilla. Fill muffin tins 2/3 full then bake 20-30 minutes, or until lightly browned.

Super Raspberry Banana Muffins

2	cups flour	3	bananas (overripe)
1/2	teaspoons baking powder	1/4	cup sour cream
3/4	teaspoons baking soda	1	teaspoon vanilla
1/4	teaspoons salt	1	pint raspberries, washed and dried
1/4	lb. butter		
1	cup sugar	1/2	cup chopped toasted almonds (optional)
2	eggs		

Preheat oven to 350° F. Sift together flour, baking powder, baking soda, and salt. Cream butter with sugar until fluffy. Beat in eggs. Purée bananas, sour cream and vanilla. Alternately add dry ingredients in 3 additions and banana mixture in 2 additions to the egg mixture, then mix until well blended. Fold in raspberries and toasted almonds (optional). Spoon into greased muffin tins and bake for about 25 minutes or until browned and springy.

★

Cake Donut Muffins

3	cups flour	1	teaspoon salt
2/3	cup sugar	3/4	teaspoon nutmeg
1	tablespoon baking powder	1/4	teaspoon cinnamon

Place above ingredients in a large bowl and stir with a spoon.

Add:

1	cup milk	2/3	cup oil

Mix well and fill 12 muffin cups. Bake 350° F. approximately 25 minutes.

Melt 1 cup margarine or butter. Put 1 cup sugar mixed with 2 teaspoons cinnamon in a bowl. While muffins are still very warm dip tops in butter and roll in sugar mixture.

Banana Blueberry Loaf Bread

1³/4	cups flour, sifted	2	eggs
2	teaspoons baking powder	1	cup bananas, mashed
1/4	teaspoon baking soda	1	cup blueberries, fresh or frozen
1/2	teaspoon salt		
1/3	cup butter	1	teaspoon vanilla
2/3	cup sugar		

Sift together flour, baking powder, soda and salt, then set aside. Cream butter and gradually beat in sugar until light and fluffy. Beat in eggs one at a time. Add flour mixture and banana alternately in three parts. Stir in vanilla. Gently stir in blueberries. Turn into oiled 9 x 5-inch loaf pan. Bake at 350° F. for 50 minutes. Cool on wire rack.

Bubba says . . .

"You can always tell a Texan. You just can't tell him much!"

★

Glazed Lemon Loaf Bread

$1^1/2$	cups flour, sifted	2	teaspoons lemon rind, grated
$1^1/2$	teaspoons baking powder	2	eggs
1	teaspoon salt	1	cup sugar
$1/2$	cup pecans, chopped	$1/2$	cup milk
$1/3$	cup butter or margarine, melted	$1/2$	cup lemon juice
		$1/3$	cup sugar

In a medium bowl, sift together flower, baking powder and salt. Stir in pecans then set aside. In large bowl, using mixer at medium speed, beat butter, lemon rind, eggs and 1 cup sugar 2 minutes. Reduce speed to low and beat in dry ingredients alternately with milk until well blended. Pour batter into greased 9 x 5 x 3-inch loaf pan. Bake at 350° F. 50-55 minutes or until loaf is golden brown and toothpick inserted in center comes out clean. Cool in pan 10 minutes. Meanwhile, in small bowl, stir together lemon juice and 1/3 cup of sugar. With toothpick or fork, prick top of loaf. Pour lemon juice mixture over loaf. Cool completely on rack before removing from pan. Wrap in foil and let stand overnight in cool, dry place before serving. Makes 1 loaf.

French Quick Bread

$1/2$	cup warm water	$1/3$	cup butter, melted
2	tablespoons yeast	2	cups hot water
3	tablespoons sugar	6	cups flour
1	tablespoon salt		

Preheat oven to 400° F. Dissolve yeast and sugar in 1/2 cup water. In large bowl, combine salt, butter, and 2 cups water. Mix in 3 cups flour. Then add yeast mixture. Mix in last 3 cups flour and stir 5 times every 10 minutes. Shape into 2 loaves and let rise until double in size. Bake for 20 minutes or until golden brown.

★

Jalapeño Cheddar Bread

2	envelopes active dry yeast	1/4	cup jalapeño peppers, minced
1	teaspoon granulated sugar	1	tablespoon salt
1/2	cup warm water	2	teaspoons Tabasco sauce
8 3/4	cups all-purpose flour	2	cups milk
3	cups extra-sharp cheddar cheese, shredded	4	large eggs

Preheat oven to 375° F. In a small bowl stir yeast, sugar, and warm water and let stand 5 minutes until foamy. Next, in a large bowl combine 8 cups flour, cheddar cheese, jalapeño pepper, salt and Tabasco pepper sauce. In a small sauce pan heat the milk over low heat until warm. Stir into flour mixture. In a medium bowl lightly beat eggs and set aside 1 tablespoon beaten egg to brush on dough later. Add remaining eggs to flour mixture and stir until the mixture makes a soft dough. On a lightly floured surface, knead remaining 3/4 cup flour into dough for about 5 minutes or until smooth and elastic. Shape the dough into a ball and place in a large, greased bowl, burning dough over to grease the top. Cover with a towel and let rise in a warm place for about 1-1/2 hours or until doubled in size. Grease two large cookie sheets. Punch down dough and divide in half. Shape each half of dough into a ball and place the balls on the cookie sheets. Cover with a towel and let rise in a warm place about 1-1/2 hours or until doubled in size. Brush the loaves with the reserved beaten egg and bake loaves about 45 minutes or until loaves sound hollow hen lightly tapped. Remove to wire racks to cool.

Bubba was . . .

driving home from his local "blue collar country club" late one night when a policeman pulled him over. The policeman asked, "Didn't you see those arrows back there?" Bubba answered, "Heck, I didn't even see the indians!"

★

Cherry Almond Coffee Cake

2	cups all-purpose flour	2	large eggs
1	teaspoon baking powder	1	teaspoon vanilla extract
1	teaspoon baking soda	1/2	teaspoon almond extract
1/2	teaspoon salt	1	cup sour cream
1/2	cup unsalted butter, room temp.	1	cup cherry pie filling
1	cup granulated sugar	1/2	cup sliced almonds, unblanched

Preheat oven to 350° F. and grease an 8 inch springform pan. Put flour, baking powder, baking soda and salt into a bowl and stir well. Beat butter in an electric mixer until creamy. Add sugar, about 1/4 cup at a time, beating after each addition. When mixture is light and fluffy, add eggs, one at a time, beating after each. Beat in extracts and remember to scrape down sides of bowl. With mixer on low, add flour mixture, about 1/2 cup at a time, alternating with sour cream, about 1/3 cup at a time, beating just until batter is smooth. Spoon half the batter into a prepared pan, then add half the cherry pie filling and swirl it through batter with a rubber spatula. Spoon remaining batter evenly over top. Spoon on remaining cherry pie filling but don't swirl. Sprinkle with almonds and press almonds lightly into surface. Bake 60 minutes or until cake is brown on top and a wooden toothpick inserted in center comes out clean. Cool in pan on wire rack 15 minutes then remove pan sides. Serve cake warm.

Corn Fritters

1	cup cornmeal	1	egg
1 1/4	cup flour	1	small can whole kernel corn, drained
1/2	teaspoon baking soda		
2	teaspoons baking powder	2	tablespoons finely chopped onion
2	teaspoons salt		
3/4	cup buttermilk	1/3	cup sugar
			Oil to fry

This is a "dump" recipe. Drop by spoonsful into hot oil and fry golden brown – drain.

★

Basic Coffee Cake

1/2	lb (2 sticks) butter, room temp.	2	teaspoons baking powder
1	cup sugar	1	teaspoon baking soda
3	eggs	1	teaspoon salt
1 1/2	teaspoons vanilla extract	1	cup sour cream
2 1/2	cups all-purpose flour	1	teaspoon vanilla

Preheat the oven to 350° F. and grease and flour a bundt pan or 10-inch tube pan. Put the butter in a large mixing bowl and beat for several seconds. Add the sugar and beat until light and fluffy. Add the eggs one at a time beating well after each. Beat in vanilla extract. Sift the flour, baking powder, baking soda, and salt into a bowl. With the mixer on low, add some flour mixture (about 3/4 cup at a time), alternating with some sour cream (about 1/3 cup at a time) beating just until smooth. Stir in vanilla. Spoon the batter into the pan and bake for about 50 minutes, or until a toothpick inserted into the center comes out clean. Remove from the oven and let rest for 5 minutes in the pan. Invert onto a rack and cool a little bit before slicing. Serve warm.

Light Potato Rolls

2	medium white potatoes	1	tablespoon sugar
1	package yeast cake	2	eggs
4	tablespoons butter	6	cups flour
2	tablespoons salt		

Preheat oven to 350° F. Boil potatoes until tender. Strain potatoes and save 1-1/4 cups potato water. Mash potatoes, then add butter, sugar and salt. When potato and potato water are lukewarm, add yeast in water and combine with potato mixture, then beat well. Sift in flour, constantly beating. Knead dough until smooth and spongy. Return to greased bowl and cover with damp cloth in a dry area. Let rise about 3 hours or until doubled in size. Turn out onto floured board and roll 1 inch thick. Cut into rounds with biscuit cutter and place on buttered sheet far apart from one another. Let rise until light. Bake until golden brown, then brush with butter and serve at once.

Homemade Cinnamon-Raisin Rolls

ROLLS

2¼	cup all-purpose flour	¹/₂	teaspoon salt
1	package active dry years	1	egg
1	cup milk	3	egg whites
¹/₄	cup margarine	2¼	cup whole-wheat flour
¹/₄	cup granulated sugar		

FILLING

¹/₂	cup dark brown sugar, firmly packed	¹/₄	cup margarine
¹/₄	cup all-purpose flour	³/₄	cup raisins (optional)
1	tablespoon ground cinnamon		Nonstick cooking spray

To make rolls, combine all-purpose flour and yeast in a large mixing bowl and set aside. In a small saucepan over low heat, combine milk, margarine, sugar and salt. Stir just until the margarine starts to melt. Add to the flour and yeast mixture, mixing well. Add egg and egg whites to the flour mixture and beat with an electric mixer on low speed for 30 seconds, continuously scraping sides of bowl. Beat on high speed for 3 minutes. Using a spoon, stir in as much of the whole-wheat flour as you can. Turn the dough onto a lightly floured surface and knead in flour for about 4 minutes or until dough is smooth and pliable. Shape into a ball and place in a bowl sprayed with a nonstick cooking spray. Turn ball over once and allow to rise in warm place 1 hour or until almost double in size.

To make filling, combine brown sugar, flour and cinnamon in a medium bowl and mix well. Cut in margarine with a pastry blender until crumbly then set aside.

Punch dough down and turn onto a lightly floured surface. Cover and let stand 10 minutes. Roll dough out into a 12-inch square and spread filling evenly over the dough. Top with raisins and roll up tightly like a jelly roll. Pinching to seal the seam. Cut roll into eight 1-1/2 -inch slices and arrange slices, cut side up, in a 9 x 13-inch baking dish sprayed with nonstick cooking spray. Cover the dish loosely with clear plastic wrap and allow to rise again about 45 minutes or until almost double in size.

★

Preheat oven to 375° F. Bake uncovered for 25 to 30 minutes or until lightly brown. If the rolls start to get too brown, cover them with foil for last 5 to 10 minutes of baking. Allow to cool 2 minutes after baking, then invert onto a wire rack and allow to cool slightly. Invert them again onto a serving dish. Serve warm or allow to cool to room temperature and freeze for future use.

Corn & Green Chile Muffins

1^1/$_2$	cup yellow cornmeal	2	large eggs, beaten
^{1}/$_2$	cup flour	1	cup sour cream
^{1}/$_2$	teaspoon onion salt	^{1}/$_4$	cup melted butter
1	tablespoon baking powder	1	12 oz. can whole kernel
1	teaspoon sugar		corn, drained
^{1}/$_2$	teaspoon salt	1	cup grated Cheddar cheese
^{1}/$_4$	teaspoon cracked black pepper	^{1}/$_2$	cup chopped canned green chilies

Mix dry ingredients well in large bowl. Add the rest of the ingredients and mix until all is moistened. Plece in well greased muffin tins and bake 25-30 minutes on 350° F.

Bubba's Beer Bread

3	cup self-rising flour	1	12-oz. can beer
^{1}/$_2$	teaspoon salt	^{1}/$_4$	cup melted butter
3	tablespoons sugar		

Combine flour, salt, sugar and beer. Spray a 9 x 5-inch bread pan and spread dough in pan. Bake 350° F. for 40-50 minutes. Remove from pan and pour melted butter over bread evenly. Bake another 10 minutes.

Bubba says . . .
"Don't call him 'cowboy' 'til you see him ride."

Poppy Seed Rolls

ROLLS

2	envelopes active dry years	1/2	cup butter
1/2	cup warm water	2	eggs
1 1/2	cups all-purpose flour	2	egg yolks, reserve egg whites
3/4	cups sugar	1/2	cup sour cream
1/2	teaspoon salt	1	teaspoon vanilla

POPPY SEED FILLING

2	tablespoons butter	2	egg whites
10	ozs. poppy seeds, coarsely ground	1/2	cup sugar
2	tablespoons honey	1/4	cup raisins (soaked in hot water until soft)
2	teaspoons lemon juice		

ICING

1	cup powdered sugar	2	tablespoons lemon juice

Beat eggs and extra yolks, then mix with yeast and stir into the flour mixture. Add the sour cream and vanilla and mix well. Knead dough on floured surface for 5 minutes. Divide in half and roll each half into a 12 inch square and cover.

To make filling, melt butter in a large pan. Add poppy seed and stir-fry for 3 minutes. Add honey, lemon juice and raisins to poppy seeds then cover and remove from heat. Let stand for 10 minutes. Beat egg whites with sugar until stiff moist peaks form. Gently fold in poppy seed mixture.

Spread half of the filling on each uncovered dough square. Roll up like a jelly-roll and seal the edges. Place on greased baking sheets and cover. Let rise 1-1/2 hours or until doubled in size.

Preheat oven to 350° F. and bake about 45 minutes, then remove from oven and cool.

To make the icing, mix powdered sugar and lemon juice until smooth then spread mixture evenly over the rolls.

★

Westfest Kolache Recipe

KOLACHE DOUGH

2	envelopes active dry yeast
1/4	cup lukewarm water
1	tablespoon sugar
1	can evaporated milk with enough water added to make 2 cups
3/4	cup butter

3/4	cup sugar
2	teaspoons salt
4	egg yolks plus one whole egg, slightly beaten
6 1/4	cups sifted flour
	Softened butter as needed

TOPPING

1	cup flour
1/2	cup sugar

1/4	cup butter or margarine

POPPY SEED FILLING – Mix well:

1	can poppy seeds
1/4	cup vanilla wavers, crushed

1/4	cup finely chopped pecans
1/2	cup honey

CREAM CHEESE FILLING – Mix well.

8	ozs. cream cheese
2	egg yolks

1/4	cup sugar
1	tablespoon lemon juice

Preheat oven to 425° F. In a small bowl dissolve yeast in warm water, sprinkle with 1 tablespoon sugar and let stand. Scald milk in sauce pan, then remove from heat and stir in butter and 1/2 cup sugar then cool to lukewarm. Add salt and egg yolks. Combine milk mixture to yeast in large bowl. Gradually add the flour until all has been used. Knead dough on lightly floured board until glossy. Place in bowl, cover to let rise in warm place 1 hour or until doubled in size.Using a tablespoon, take egg-sized bits of the dough and roll into balls on a floured board. Place on greased baking sheet about 1 inch apart, brush each with softened butter, and let rise again, covered, until light. Make an indentation in each, large enough to hold 1 teaspoon of fruit filling. Sprinkle fruit with some of the topping. Bake for 15 minutes. Remove from oven and brush with softened butter immediately. Cool kolaches on wire rack

Makes about 3-1/2 dozen.

★

Texas Tidbit

There is a belief in Texas, even amongst well educated people, that former Governor James (Jim) Hogg named two daughters Ima and Ura, thus, making them Ima Hogg and Ura Hogg. Actually and factually there was no Ura Hogg, but he certainly did have a daughter named Miss Ima Hogg. Jim Hogg served as governor of Texas from January 20, 1891 through January 15, 1895 being reelected in 1892. He was the "farmer's friend."

Miss Ima showered the city of Houston with invaluable gifts too numerous to mention. Just one of the gifts is the Houston Symphony Orchestra. I believe Miss Ima died at the age of 93 while leaving Harrods department store in London.

A Typical Texas Breakfast in 1890
by Mrs. James S. Hogg
(Always served promptly at 7:00 AM)

A small bowl of clabber (for the children)
OR oatmeal with thick cream (We always had 2 Hereford cows and a calf.)
Home-cured ham, sliced and fried
Grits with red gravy
Eggs fried on one side
Butter biscuits or cornmeal batter cakes with Ribbon cane syrup

A real treat was cold biscuits split and buttered with molasses and toasted in the oven until candied.

Among other things that were served at receptions were rosettes. It is not difficult to procure the rosette iron at this time and the recipe is enclosed with the irons.

– Mrs. James S. Hogg

★ *I ran across this by accident in my recipe files, therefore I cannot give credit where credit is due. I don't know where I got it or from whom, but I find it a great piece of Texas history. The Hogg family was very colorful for the times. It sounds as if Mrs. Hogg either had very good help or was awfully busy. I can't imagine what lunch and dinner must have been if this was breakfast! This must sound very ambitious to our young ladies of today. . . .D.G.*

★

The Whole Hogg

(And Other Main Dishes)

Skillet Goulash

(Great with cornbread)

1/2	lbs ground beef	1/2	teaspoon cracked pepper
1	large chopped onion	1/2	teaspoon chili powder
1	small can diced tomatoes	2	cups cook macaroni
1	medium can tomato sauce	1/4	cup parmesan
1	teaspoon garlic salt		

Brown beef and onion then add all other ingredients except macaroni and simmer 30 minutes. Add macaroni and simmer 15 minutes. Top with cheese and just serve it from the skillet for a great "stove dinner"! Serves 4-6 people

For leftovers, add a small can of tomato sauce and a little water when reheating.

Pepper Steak

2	lbs. sirloin, cut into 1/4" strips	2	tablespoons butter
2-3	bell peppers, sliced into strips	3	garlic cloves, minced
6	sliced green onions (with tops)	1 1/2	tablespoons paprika
2	large, firm tomatoes, peeled and diced	2	tablespoons soy sauce
1	cup beef broth	4	cups hot cooked rice
1/4	cup water	1/2	teaspoon cracked pepper
2	tablespoons cornstarch	1/2	teaspoon salt

Sprinkle steak with paprika, pepper and salt. Sauté steak and garlic in butter until brown. Add green pepper and onion. Cook vegies half way done. Add tomatoes and broth. Cover and simmer 20 minutes. Whisk cornstarch, water and soy sauce. Stir into steak mixture and cook uncovered until thickened. Serve over fluffy white rice.

Serves 8

"Manly" Meat Loaf

2	lbs. ground meat	1½	teaspoon salt
3	slices white bread (crust removed)	1½	teaspoon cayenne pepper
1	cup corn flakes	2	tablespoons Worcestershire sauce
1	cup chopped onion	1	cup chicken broth, canned
2	garlic cloves, chopped finely	1	teaspoon sugar

Preheat oven to 350° F. Mix all ingredients together in large bowl and let stand 15 minutes. Mix again and form loaf in a 5 x 9 baking dish. Bake 1 hour, 15 minutes or until done. Let stand 10 minutes before slicing with spatula.

Serves 5-6

Salisbury Steak with Mushroom Gravy

SALISBURY STEAK

1	lb. lean ground beef	1	tablespoon prepared horseradish
⅓	cup finely chopped onion		
¼	cup saltine cracker crumbs	¼	teaspoon salt
1	egg white, slightly beaten	⅛	teaspoon pepper
2	tablespoons milk		

MUSHROOM GRAVY

1	jar (12 oz.) brown beef gravy	4	oz. mushrooms, sliced
2	tablespoons water		

In medium bowl, combine Salisbury Steak ingredients, mixing lightly but thoroughly. Shape into 4 half-inch thick oval patties. Heat large non-stick skillet on medium. Place patties in skillet and cook 7 to 8 minutes or until no longer pink and juices run clear (turn once). Remove from skillet and keep warm.

In same skillet, combine gravy ingredients and cook over medium heat 3 to 5 minutes or until mushrooms are tender. Serve over Salisbury Steak.

Serves 4

Peppercorn Beef Kabobs

1	lb. boneless beef sirloin steak cut 1 inch thick	1	clove garlic, crushed
1¹/₂	teaspoons black peppercorns, crushed	1	medium onion, cut into 12 wedges
¹/₂	teaspoon each salt and pepper		Cherry tomato haves, optional

Combine peppercorns, salt, paprika and garlic in shallow dish. Coat beef with mixture. Thread an equal number of beef pieces onto each of four 12-inch skewers along with three onion wedges. Place kabobs on rack in broiler pan so surface of meat is 3 to 4 inches from heat. Broil 9 to 12 minutes for rare to medium, turning occasionally.

Serves 2-3

Easy Beef & Salsa Burritos

1	lb. lean ground beef	1	pkg. (10 oz.) frozen chopped spinach, defrosted, well drained
1	tablespoon chili powder		
¹/₄	teaspoon ground cumin		
¹/₄	teaspoon salt	³/₄	cup shredded Colby Jack cheese
¹/₄	teaspoon pepper		
1	cup prepared chunky salsa	8	medium flour tortillas, warmed

Spray large skillet, then brown ground beef over medium heat 8 to 10 minutes or until no longer pink. Pour off drippings. Season beef with chili powder, cumin, salt and pepper. Stir in spinach and salsa; heat through. Remove from heat and stir in cheese. Spoon 1/2 cup beef mixture in center of each tortilla. Fold bottom edge up over filling and fold sides to center so they are overlapping.

Serves 4-6

Easy Beef Stroganoff

1	lb beef round tip steaks, cut 1/8" to 1/4" thick	1/4	teaspoon pepper
4	cups (5 oz.) uncooked wide egg noodles	1/2	lb. sliced mushrooms
		1	pkg. (3/4 ox.) onion soup mix
4	teaspoons vegetable oil, divided	1	cup cold water
1	clove garlic, crushed	1/4	cup dairy sour cream

Cook noodles according to package directions; keep warm. Stack beef steaks. Cut lengthwise in half and then crosswise into 1-inch wide strips. In large non-stick skillet, heat 2 teaspoons oil on medium. Add beef and garlic (1/2 at a time) and stir-fry 1 minute or until outside surface of beef is no longer pink. (Do not overcook.) Remove from skillet and season with salt and pepper. In same skillet, cook mushrooms in remaining 2 teaspoons oil 2 minutes or until tender, stirring occasionally. Remove from heat. Add onion mix and water; blend well. Return to heat; bring to a boil. Reduce heat to low and simmer 1 minute or until sauce is thickened. Stir frequently. Return beef to skillet and heat thoroughly. Stir in sour cream. Serve over noodles.

Serves 4.

Another Beef Stroganoff

2	lbs. round steak, cut into narrow strips	2	5 oz. cans button mushrooms drained
2	tablespoons oil	1/3	teaspoon small cracked pepper
1	cup water		
1	package onion soup mix	1	cup sour cream
2	small cans cream of mushroom soup		Cooked rice or noodles

Brown steak in oil. Add water and onion soup mix and simmer, covered, 45 minutes very slowly. Add soup, mushrooms and pepper. Simmer 10 minutes. Add sour cream just before serving. Stir in well. Serve over cooked noodles or rice.

Serves 6-8.

Burgundy Beef & Vegetable Stew

1¹/₂	lbs. beef eye round	3	large cloves garlic, crushed
1	tablespoon vegetable oil	1¹/₂	cups baby carrots
1	teaspoon dried thyme leaves	1	cup frozen whole pearl onions
¹/₂	teaspoon salt	1¹/₂	tablespoon cornstarch,
¹/₂	teaspoon pepper		dissolved in 1 tablespoon
1	13³/₄-oz. can ready-to-serve		water
	broth	1	package (8 ozs.) frozen
¹/₂	cup Burgundy wine		green peas

Tim fat from beef; and cut into 1-inch pieces. In Dutch oven, heat oil on medium. Add beef (half at a time) and brown evenly, stirring occasionally. Pour off drippings. Season with thyme, salt and pepper. Stir in broth, wine and garlic. Bring to a boil, then reduce heat to low. Cover tightly and simmer 1-1/2 hours. Add carrots and onions. Cover and continue cooking 35 to 40 minutes or until beef and vegetables are tender. Bring beef stew to a boil on medium. Add cornstarch mixture, then cook and stir 1 minute. Stir in green peas. Reduce heat to medium and cook 3 to 4 minutes or until peas are heated through.

Serves 6-8.

Beef Hash

4	cups chopped leftover roast	¹/₂	teaspoon chili powder
1	large onion, chopped	3	tablespoons flour
	(or 2 smaller onions)	3	potatoes, chopped bite-sized
3-4	cups beef bouillon		Salt and pepper to taste
2	tablespoon margarine		

Sauté onions in 2 tablespoons margarine. Then place roast in pot with bouillon and onion. Simmer 30 minutes. Whisk flour and chili powder into a half cup cold water and add to the pot. Stir and add the potatoes, salt and pepper. Simmer another 30 minutes.

Serves 6.

Bubba's Beef Stew

3	lbs roast, cubed	1¹/₂	cups beef broth
¹/₃	cup flour	1	can beer
¹/₃	cup oil	¹/₂	teaspoon chili powder
3	potatoes, peeled & quartered	1	small can tomato sauce
3	onions, quartered	1	tablespoon vinegar
4	cloves garlic, minced	¹/₄	cup flour
³/₄	cup frozen green peas		Salt and pepper to taste
6	carrots, cut into 2-inch lengths		

Coat the beef cubes in 1/3 cup flour, salt and pepper them and sear in 1/3 cup oil until about half way done. Then drain meat and place in roaster. Put all the rest of the ingredients into the roaster and place in a 350° F. oven for 3 hours. Take out 2 cups broth and whisk 1/4 cup flour into it. Taste the broth from the roaster for salt and pepper level now. Adjust. Now pour this mixture back and stir well. Bake another hour.

Serves 8-10.

Bubba says . . .

"He doesn't eat cured meat anymore. Cured from what? Bubonic plague? He thinks there should be a disclosure on the meat package, cured from _____ ."

★

Top of the Stove
Bourbon Rib Eyes with Grilled Mushrooms
(I'll just talk you through it!)

1/4	cups bourbon whiskey	3	cups sliced mushrooms
2	large rib eye steaks to die for	4	green onions, finely chopped

In a very large skillet place 1 tablespoon margarine to heat. Sprinkle your steaks with small cracked pepper and garlic salt. Be the generous person I know you are! Sear the steaks over a higher heat than you intend to grill them – about two minutes each side. Lower your burner. Slice 3 cups mushrooms and finely chopped green onions. Throw another tablespoon of margarine on the skillet and turn the steaks. Place the mushrooms and onions all around and garlic salt and pepper them. Now we're cookin'! Drizzle 1/4 cup whiskey all over everything. Sauté the mushrooms and turn the steaks until they're the correct amount of doneness for you. Turn up the burner and quickly finish sautéing the mushrooms. Pour over the steaks and make sure you get all the juice. With a salad and baked potato I'd say you're in business! I like to add bell pepper strips to this occasionally.

Serves 2 lucky people.

Bubba says . . .

"Trap it, stab it, shoot it, club it, stomp it or hook it and then FRY it!"

★

The Steer's Rear

Place a large rump roast in a large covered pot or small roaster with lid. Place water 2/3 of the way up the roast. Add 1 box (2 pkgs.) Lipton's Onion Soup Mix, 1/4 cup vinegar, 1/2 teaspoon Worcestershire, 1/2 teaspoon chili powder, 1/2 teaspoon celery salt, 1/2 teaspoon teaspoon garlic powder and 1/2 teaspoon small cracked pepper.

Place covered roaster in preheated 400° F. oven for 1 hour. Reduce heat to 250° F. and bake for about 10 hours. You don't even need to peek. Don't forget to use the lid and cover well.

Remove lid and remove roast to a platter. Add 1/4 cup flour to liquid and whisk well until it is smooth. Taste and adjust salt and pepper if necessary. Pour gravy over roast.I suggest mashed potatoes and peas & carrots with this roast.

Serves 6-8

If you have leftovers try cubing the meat and placing the meat and gravy in a large saucepan. Throw in the rest of the peas & carrots and add 2 cups cooked, cubed potatoes, drained. Add 1 teaspoon chili powder and heat. Stir well, but don't break up potatoes. Serve with cornbread. This is sort of a combination of hash and stew.

Whiskey River Pork Tenderloins

2	lbs pork tenderloin	1/4	cup olive oil
1/4	cup bourbon whiskey	2	teaspoons Worcestershire
1/4	cups soy sauce	4	cloves garlic, minced
1/4	cup brown sugar	1	pkg. onion soup mix
1/4	cup Dijon mustard	1/2	teaspoon cracked pepper

Place tenderloins in a large pyrex dish and mix and put the rest of the ingredients over them. Turn several times. Cover and refrigerate overnight. Bake tenderloins, covered, in a 400° F. oven for 30 minutes. Reduce heat to 300° F. and bake for several hours. Remove lid and bake until golden. Baste and serve.

Serves 5-6

★

Honey Roasted Pork Chops

8	butterflied pork chops	1/4	teaspoon onion salt
1/3	cups honey	1/4	teaspoon thyme
2	tablespoons Dijon mustard	1/4	teaspoon salt
1/4	teaspoon garlic pepper		

Sear the pork chops in a greased pan 3 minutes on each side. Mix all other ingredients together and brush on both sides of meat. Place chops and the honey mixture in a baking bag and bake 1 hour in a 300° F. oven.

Serves 5-6

Meat Balls & Spaghetti
VERY SPICY!

SAUCE

2	cans Rotel tomatoes (10 oz.)	1/3	cup oil
2	cans tomato sauce (7 oz.)	6	bay leaves
2	cans whole tomatoes (medium sized)	1/3	cup sugar
3	cups chopped onion	1	teaspoon salt
1	teaspoon minced garlic	1	teaspoon cayenne pepper

Put all ingredients in pot and bring to boil. Boil 20 minutes on high, stirring constantly. Lower heat to medium, cover pot and cook 1-1/2 hours. Stir often.

MEATBALLS

1 1/2	lbs. ground beef	1	cup chopped onion
1	teaspoon salt	1/3	cup grated parmesan cheese
1/2	teaspoon cayenne pepper	1	teaspoon flour
1	cup corn flakes	1	can beef broth
2	eggs		

Mix all ingredients together. Oil hands and roll out meatballs. Bake in pan at 375° F. until slightly brown. Turn and brown other side. Add to sauce above. In a bowl, dissolve flour in beef broth than add to meatball drippings. Stir then add to sauce. Cook additional 15 minutes on medium. Serve over boiled spaghetti.

★

Stuffed Jumbo Pasta Shells

24	jumbo pasta shells, boiled and drained		2	cups milk
6	tablespoons butter		1	cup heavy cream
6	garlic cloves, peeled and finely chopped		1/2	cup finely chopped parsley
6	tablespoons flour		6	anchovy fillets, finely chopped
			A little salt	

CHEESE AND PROSCIUTTO STUFFING

500	gm ricotta cheese		3	tablespoons chopped parsley
250	gm cottage cheese		3	tablespoons chopped fresh basil
1/4	cup grated Parmesan			
6	thin slices prosciutto, cut into tiny squares		2	egg yolks, beaten
			Salt and pepper to taste	

Melt the butter in a heavy-bottomed saucepan over low heat. Add the garlic and sauté until barely golden brown. Remove from heat and add flour when butter stops bubbling. Return to the heat and cook 2 minutes, stirring constantly. Do not let the flour color! Remove from the heat and add the milk and cream all at once. Immediately beat vigorously with a whisk until smooth. Put the pan over medium heat and add the parsley and anchovies. Cook, stirring constantly until the sauce has the constancy of heavy cream. Remove from the heat and salt and pepper to taste. Reserve uncovered.

In a large bowl, combine the ricotta, cottage cheese, Parmesan, parsley, basil, prosciutto and egg yolks. Add salt and pepper to taste, and mix well.

Stuff each shell with some of the cheese mixture. Using your fingers, to maintain the shape of the shell as it was before boiling. Wipe off excess filling.

Put about two cups of the sauce in the bottom of a baking dish big enough to hold all the 24 shells in one layer. Place the stuffed shells in the dish and pour the remaining sauce over. Bake in a preheated oven at 375° F. for 15 minutes then serve immediately.

Serves 6-8.

Pasta Pie

1	lb. ground beef	1	small can tomato sauce (or
2	lbs. ricotta cheese		larger, depending on taste)
1	pkg. non-spaghetti pasta		Garlic and oregano to taste

Brown meat and spices. Boil water for pasta then cook pasta until al dente. Mix meat and cheese and add cooked pasta. Spread evenly throughout pan. Drizzle tomato sauce on top and bake for 20 or 30 minutes at 350° F. until cheese begins to brown or sauce starts to bubble.

Penne Pasta with Tomato Cream Sauce

6	oz. penne pasta, uncooked	1	teaspoon sugar
	Vegetable cooking spray	$1/2$	teaspoon dried basil
4	oz. Canadian bacon, chopped	$1/4$	teaspoon freshly ground
$3/4$	cup chopped sweet red pepper		pepper
$1/4$	cup chopped onion	$1/4$	teaspoon salt
1	clove garlic, minced	2	teaspoon all-purpose flour
1	(14-1/2 oz.) can whole peeled	$1/4$	cup evaporated skimmed milk
	tomatoes (no-salt) undrained		
	and chopped		

Cook pasta according to package directions, then drain and set aside. Coat a large non-stick skillet with cooking spray and place over medium-high heat until hot. Add the Canadian bacon, red pepper, onion and garlic, then sauté until vegetables are tender. Add tomato and the next four ingredients. Bring mixture to a boil. Cover, reduce heat, and simmer 10 more minutes. Add pasta, stirring well. Cook over medium heat 2 to 3 minutes or until thoroughly heated. Transfer mixture to a serving bowl. Garnish with a basil spring if desired.

★

Chicken Spaghetti

12	oz. cooked spaghetti	1	tablespoon flour
1	tablespoon unsalted butter	1 1/2	cup unsalted chicken stock
2	tablespoons bacon drippings	3	ripe tomatoes
1	large onion, chopped	1/4	cup chili sauce
3	celery stalks, chopped	3/4	cup half & half
1	green bell pepper, chopped	2	tablespoons parsley, minced
1	cup mushrooms, minced	2	cups diced chicken, cooked
3	garlic cloves, minced	1/2	cup sliced pimento-stuffed
1	teaspoon Worcestershire sauce		olives
2	teaspoons chili powder	2	cups grated mild cheddar cheese

Preheat oven to 350° F. and grease large baking dish. Toss spaghetti with butter and set aside. Warm bacon drippings in skillet over medium heat. Cook onion, celery, bell pepper, mushrooms, garlic, Worcestershire and chili powder until vegetables are softened, about 15 minutes. Sprinkle in flour and add stock, tomatoes and chili sauce. Bring to boil, reduce to simmer and cook 30 minutes, or until thickened. Remove from heat and add half & half and parsley. Pour over spaghetti and toss well. Place half of spaghetti and sauce in dish, then top with half each of chicken, olives and cheese. Add remaining spaghetti, then the rest of the chicken, olives and cheese. Bake 25 minutes or until bubbly.

Serves a crowd.

★ *Chicken Spaghetti serves a lot of Texas crowds from church functions to dinner parties to just about any function. It stretches well.*

Baked Chicken Parmesan

5	tablespoons melted unsalted butter	2	tablespoons fresh parsley, chopped
1	tablespoons Dijon or dry mustard	1	teaspoon dried basil
1/2	cup freshly grated Parmesan cheese	3	whole chicken breasts, bone, split
		3/4	cup dried bread crumbs

Perheat the oven to 400° F. and lightly grease a 9" x 15" baking dish. In a shallow bowl, combine the butter with the mustard. In another shallow bowl, blend together the bread crumbs, cheese, parsley, and basil. Dip the chicken pieces first into the mustard mixture, then coat with the bread crumb mixture. Place skin side up in the baking dish and bake uncovered for 45 minutes.

Serves 4-6.

South of the Border Fried Chicken

Run over 1 chicken. Sell it to the nearest restaurant. It picks up like a slinky, but with the right recipe it's not bad! Especially after all those margaritas.

1	cup milk	Salt and pepper to taste
2	beaten eggs	

Beat milk and eggs together. Dip washed and dried chicken pieces that have been salted and peppered in milk/egg mixture.

Then roll in flour and repeat.

Fry in heated oil until golden brown, turning once.

Luckenbach **Lemon Chicken**

1 lb. chicken breasts, skinned & boned

BATTER

2	tablespoons white flour	1/4	teaspoon salt
1/2	teaspoon baking powder	2	tablespoons water
1/2	teaspoons cornflour	4	fluid oz. oil for frying
1	egg		

LEMON SAUCE

2	tablespoons lemon juice	1	scant teaspoon salt
1	lemon, cut in thin slices		White pepper to taste
5	tablespoons rich chicken broth	1	scant teaspoon cornflour mixed with
1	teaspoon rice wine or dry sherry	1	scant teaspoon water
1	tablespoon sugar	1 1/2	teaspoons sesame oil

Lightly pound chicken. Combine all the batter ingredients together in a medium sized bowl and mix well. Add the flattened chicken and coat thoroughly. Heat a wok until hot and add the oil. Fry the chicken pieces on medium about 2 minutes per side or until they are brown and crisp. Drain on paper towels. Drain the wok and wipe clean. Add the lemon sauce ingredients and simmer for 2 minutes. Meanwhile cut the chicken into bite-sized pieces and arrange on a serving plate. Pour the sauce over the chicken and serve at once.

Serves 2-3.

★ *Luckenbach is a tiny, tiny Texas town that has received a lot of fame by the song "Let's Go To Luckenbach, Texas" – It talks about Waylon and Willie and the boys. Don't blink driving through Luckenbach or you'll miss it!*

★

Brazos Valley Baked Chicken Breasts

2	tablespoons of butter or margarine	1/2	cup dry sherry
2	tablespoons of salad oil	1	teaspoon tarragon leaves
6	skinless/boneless chicken breasts	1	teaspoon Worcestershire sauce
1	can of condensed cream of chicken soup	1/2	teaspoon chervil leaves
1/2	cup light cream	1/4	teaspoon garlic powder
		1	can (6 oz.) or 1 pkg. of sliced mushrooms, drained

Heat oven to 350° F. In oven, heat butter and oil in 9 x 12 baking dish until butter is melted. Place chicken in baking dish, turning to coat with butter, then bake uncovered for one hour. Ten minutes before chicken is done, heat soup, cream and wine, stirring occasionally. Stir in tarragon leaves, Worcestershire sauce, chervil leaves, garlic powder and mushrooms. Remove chicken from oven, drain fat, and pour mixture over chicken. Cover tightly and cook 15-20 minutes longer or until tender.

Serves 4-5.

Old Chisholm Trail Garlic-Ginger Roasted Chicken

1 whole chicken or 4 breasts (boneless)

MARINADE

1/2	cup soy sauce	2	tablespoons garlic, minced
1/4	cup honey	2	tablespoons ginger root, minced
1/4	cup vinegar (any type)		

Place your rinsed chicken in a Ziploc bag and cover with marinade. Make sure there is no air inside when Ziploc is sealed. Marinate at least 8 hours, preferably overnight. When ready to roast, place breast side down in a shallow pan. Roast about 20-25 minutes. Turn the chicken breast side up during the last half hour. Chicken should be dark brown when done. Watch carefully as the marinade tends to scorch.

Serves 3-4.

★

Jalapeño Chicken Breasts

Good recipe!

6   chicken breasts, skinned and cut in half
1/4   cup lime juice
2   tablespoons finely chopped onion
1/4   cup honey
1/4   cup soy sauce

2   tablespoons chopped cilantro
3   jalapeños, seeded, finely chopped
3   garlic cloves, minced
2   cups grated Monterey Jack cheese
1   tablespoon chopped cilantro

Mix together all ingredients, except Monterey Jack cheese and 1 tablespoon cilantro, and pour over chicken, turning chicken to marinate. Marinate overnight in a pyrex baking dish. Grill the chicken breasts in a large saucepan well sprayed with until done. Place breasts in the same dish you marinated in. Put 2 cups grated Monterey Jack cheese over breasts and bake 20 minutes on 325° F. Garnish with cilantro.

Serves 4-5.

Jalapeño Chili

6   lbs. chili meat
4   onions, chopped

6   garlic cloves, minced
4   jalapeños, minced, no seeds

Brown above in 1/4 cup oil, drain and add:

1   large can tomatoes, cut up
1   quart water
1   12-oz. can tomato paste
1   can beef broth
1   teaspoon cumin
2   teaspoons cayenne pepper
2   teaspoons Tabasco

1/2   cup chili powder
1   teaspoon paprika
1   teaspoon oregano
1   teaspoon salt
1   beer (whatever you're drinking)

Stir well and simmer for 1 hour stirring occasionally. Remove lid and "cook down" stirring for another 29 minutes or so.

Comanche Chili

Fry 4 slices bacon very crisp and set aside to drain. In the bacon grease brown:

3	lbs. ground beef		1	minced bell pepper
3	large chopped onions		4	garlic cloves, minced

Drain and add:

1/4	cup chili powder		1	teaspoon cayenne
1	can tomato sauce, 15-oz.		2	teaspoons salt
1	can tomato paste, 6 oz.		1/4	teaspoon pepper
1	teaspoon paprika OR			(small cracked)
	red pepper		1	quart water

Simmer and stir occasionally for at least an hour – 2 hours is better!

Texas Chili with Beans
(or without)

★ *Most Texans do not like beans in their chili.*

3	lbs. chili meat		4	cloves garlic, minced
2	large chopped onions		1/4	cup oil

Brown the above until light brown. Add:

1/4	cup chili powder		1/2	teaspoon cayenne
2	teaspoons salt		2	teaspoons cumin
1	can tomato sauce, 8 oz.		2	teaspoons Tabasco
1	can tomato paste, 6 oz.		1	quart water
1	can chopped green chilies		1	quart beer
1	teaspoon paprika			

Simmer 1-1/2 hours. If desired stir in 1 lb. cooked pinto beans. Simmer 1/2 hour more.

★ If you like your chili thicker, whisk 1/8 cup masa into 1 cup water and add for the last 1/2 hour.

Mexican Beef Stir Fry

1   lb. beef flank steak
2   tablespoons vegetable oil
1   teaspoon each ground cumin
    and dried oregano leaves
1   clove garlic, crushed
1   red or green bell pepper,
    cup into thin strips

1   medium onion, cut into
    thin strips
1   medium onion, cut into
    thin wedges
1-2 jalapeño peppers, thinly
    sliced
2   cups cooked rice

Cut beef steak into 1/8 inch thick strips. Combine oil, cumin, oregano and garlic. Reserve half. Heat half the seasoned oil in large non-stick skillet on medium. Add bell pepper, onion and jalapeño pepper, then stir-fry 2 to 3 minutes or until crisp and tender. Remove and reserve. In same skillet stir-fry strips (1/2 at a time) in remaining oil 1 to 2 minutes. Return vegetables to skillet and heat through. Serve beef mixture over rice.

Serves 2-3.

Cheese Enchiladas

FILLING

1¹/₂ lbs. mild cheddar cheese,
      grated
¹/₂   medium onion, finely
      chopped
1   batch Diane's "Braggin' Rights"
      Chili (page 191)

Oil for frying
12-16 corn tortillas
Grated mild cheddar cheese
and chopped onions, for garnish

Preheat oven to 350° F. and grease medium baking dish. Mix cheese with onions and set aside. Warm chili if it has been refrigerated. Heat 1/2 to 1" oil in skillet and use tongs to dunk tortillas long enough for them to go limp, just a matter of seconds. Drain tortillas. Dip tortillas in chili to lightly coat it, then lay tortilla down, sprinkle 1/4 cup filling over it, and roll it up tightly. Place enchilada in baking dish and repeat with remaining tortillas. Top enchiladas with remaining chili and bake 15-18 minutes or until chili bubbles. Remove from oven and sprinkle with cheese and onions. Serve enchiladas with a spatula.

Texas Tamale Pie

FILLING

1	lb. lean ground beef		1	tablespoon chili powder
1	medium onion, chopped		2	teaspoon cumin seeds, toasted and ground
1	green bell pepper, chopped			
2	cloves garlic, minced		1/2	teaspoon salt
1	cup corn kernels		1/2	teaspoon dried oregano
1	cup fresh tomatoes, chopped			
1/2	cup unsalted beef stock			

TOPPING

2	cups unsalted beef stock		1/2	teaspoon salt
1	can masa harina		1	egg, separated
1/2	teaspoon chili powder		1/2	cup grated cheddar cheese

Preheat oven to 350° F. Grease medium baking dish. Make filling by sautéing ground beef, onion, bell pepper and garlic until lightly browned. Drain fat. Mix in corn, tomatoes and stock. Stir in chili powder, cumin, 1/2 teaspoon salt and oregano. Cook uncovered on medium for 20 minutes or until mixture is no longer soupy. Add salt to taste.

Prepare dough topping while filling cools. Bring stock to boil in heavy saucepan and gradually add masa, stirring constantly. Stir in chili powder and salt. Reduce heat and stir 8-10 minutes until masa is stiff. Remove from heat and pour beaten egg yolk into masa. Beat egg white until stiff and fold into masa. Spoon filling in baking dish and spread batter over it. Top with grated cheese and bake 30 minutes or until lightly puffed and brown. Cut into slices and serve.

Serves 4-5.

Bubba says . . .

"If his pickup was a horse, he'd have shot it by now."

Honey Sesame Shrimp

1	cup all-purpose flour	2	tablespoons cornstarch
Pinch of salt		Oil for frying	
Pepper		1	tablespoon sesame oil
1	egg lightly beaten	2	tablespoons honey
1	lb. shrimp, shelled and deveined	2	tablespoons sesame seeds
		2/3	cup water

Sift the flour, salt, and pepper into a bowl. Make a well in the center, add the egg and water, and gradually mix in the flour. Beat until smooth then set aside for 10 minutes.

Toss shrimp in the cornstarch and coat well, shaking off excess. Add the shrimp to the batter mixture and coat well. Heat the oil in the wok and add a few shrimp at a time. Cook until the batter is golden. Remove the cooked shrimp, drain them on paper towels, and keep warm. Repeat until all the shrimp have been fried. Carefully remove the remaining hot oil from wok. Gently heat the sesame oil in pan. Add honey and stir until thoroughly mixed and heated. Add the shrimp to the mixture and toss well. Sprinkle over sesame seeds and toss well again. Serve immediately.

Serves 3-4.

★ *"Texas is a state of mind. Texas is an obsession. Above all, Texas is a nation in every sense of the word."*

– John Steinbeck

Sweet and Sour Fish

1	lb. white fish (I like halibut)	2	teaspoons cornflour
1	egg white		Pinch salt
Oil for frying			

SAUCE

1	tablespoon cornflour	1	tablespoon brown sugar
1	tablespoon soy sauce	1	tablespoon tomato puree
1	tablespoon dry sherry	1	teaspoon French mustard
1	tablespoon cider vinegar	1/2	pint fish stock

Cut fish into 1-inch cubes. Lightly beat the egg white in a shallow dish with the cornflour and salt and coat fish cubes well. Refrigerate while preparing the sauce. Blend the cornflour with 2 tablespoons of the stock until smooth, then add the remaining stock and sauce ingredients. Stir well. Pour enough oil for frying into a wok or deep pan, heat, then fry fish a few pieces at a time for 2-3 minutes or until golden brown. Drain each piece well and keep hot. Heat the sauce in another saucepan, bring to a boil, then simmer for 1-2 minutes.

Serves 2-3

Cowboys say . . .

"Always drink upstream from the buffalo!"

Orange, Orange Roughy

2	lbs. orange roughy	1/4	teaspoon pepper
2/3	cup flour	1/4	cup oil
1/2	teaspoon salt		

Wash fish and sprinkle with salt and pepper. Coat with flour and place in hot oil. Cook on each side 4 minutes. Pour orange sauce over fillets and serve immediately on a bed of pilaf.

Orange Sauce

3	cloves garlic, minced	2	tablespoons orange juice
2	tablespoons lime juice	3	tablespoons chives, minced
2	tablespoons lemon juice	1	tablespoon parsley, minced

Sauté garlic in 2 teaspoons butter over low heat for 2 minutes. Add the rest of the ingredients and boil over low heat for 2 minutes.

Serves 4-5.

Bubba says . . .

"Do you know why cowboys wear 10 gallon hats? If they get caught in a flood, they can float in them. If they get caught in a fire, they can beat it out with them. If they get caught in a lie, they can hide in them."

Egg Plant Parmesan

Try this one! It's very good.

2	tablespoons margarine	2¹/₂	cups water mixed with:	
1	large onion	¹/₈	teaspoon cayenne	
2	medium eggplants	1	teaspoon garlic salt	
1¹/₂	lbs ground meat	1	teaspoon dried Italian	
1	14¹/₂ oz. can diced tomato		spices	
1	small can tomato paste		Pinch sugar	
		¹/₄	teaspoon salt	
¹/₄	Parmesan cheese			
1	Pkg. grated Mozzarella cheese, 2 cups			
2	tablespoons Parmesan			

Peel eggplant and slice into 1-inch rings. Place on paper towels and sprinkle with 2 tablespoons salt very evenly. Leave for 1 hour to draw out bitterness. Wash eggplant and cut into 1-inch cubes. Sauté eggplant and onion and set aside. Brown ground meat, drain and add to eggplant and onion. Add all the rest of the ingredients except cheeses and mix well. Pour into a buttered dish. Top with 1/4 cup Parmesan. Bake 375° F. 30 minutes. Top with Mozzarella and sprinkle with 2 tablespoons Parmesan – Bake 8 minutes longer.

Serves 6-8.

Cowboys say . . .

"When a real cowboy rides you never see daylight between him and the saddle."

Potato Stroganoff

SAUTÉ

2-1/2 lbs. sirloin trimmed and cut into 3/4-inch cubes. Sauté until grey and medium rare. Pour water over meat, approximately 3-1/4 cups, and add 3 packages (1-1/2 boxes) of Lipton Onion Soup Mix and 1/3 to 1/2 teaspoon small cracked pepper. Cover and simmer an hour.

ADD:

2	cans cream of mushroom soup	1/4	cups cooking sherry
1	large jar sliced mushrooms	1/2	teaspoon Worcestershire

Stir well or until soup is fairly smooth. Add 1/2 cup sour cream and stir well.

Place 1 package (thawed) frozen hash browns in a large sprayed pyrex dish and pour mixture over it. Bake 400° F. 40 minutes. Reduce to 375° F. for 20 minutes.

When I make this dish I take out about 2/3 cup liquid before pouring over potatoes. When the hour baking is over, I pour the liquid on top very evenly as the rest on top tends to dry out a little.

Serves 6-8.

Huevos Rancheros

2	medium onions	6	eggs
2	green chili peppers	1	tablespoon margarine
3	fresh tomatoes	1/3	teaspoon salt
1	tablespoon parsley, minced	1/4	teaspoon pepper

Chop onion, peppers and tomatoes. Brown with parsley in butter, adding salt and pepper. Simmer 5 minutes. Fry eggs and pour this wonderful sauce over them.

Serves 3-4.

Portabello Mushroom Sandwich

MARINADE

2	tablespoons wine vinegar		2	teaspoons oregano, rubbed
2	tablespoons lemon juice		1	pinch salt
2	tablespoons olive oil		1	pinch sugar
1	clove garlic, minced		1	pinch black pepper

RECIPE

1	clove garlic		2	teaspoons balsamic vinegar
2	tablespoons mayonnaise		2	teaspoons shallots, minced
2	teaspoons thyme, chopped		2	soft onion rolls, split & grilled
2	large Portabello mushrooms		2	slices Monterey Jack cheese
1	red bell pepper, roasted, peeled, and seeded			

Combine marinade ingredients and marinate mushrooms 1 to 2 hours. Mash other garlic clove into fine paste. Stir into mayonnaise and add thyme.

Cook mushrooms 4 minutes on each side on a grill or under a broiler until soft. Sprinkle red bell pepper with balsamic vinegar and shallots. Spread mayonnaise on each half of toasted rolls. Place grilled mushrooms on two onion roll halves, cover with roasted bell pepper, cheese and top half of rolls. Serve immediately

Cowboys say . . .

"On a trail drive what can't be cured must be endured."

Pescado en Salsa Verde

(Fish in Green Sauce)

1	lb. fresh tomatillos OR
1³/4 cups drained canned tamatillos	
3	green onions, with some green tops
1	tablespoon chopped parsley leaves
1	small California chile, roasted, peeled, seeded, OR
1	canned whole green chile

1	garlic clove
2	teaspoons vegetable oil
Salt	
1¹/2	lbs. white fish fillets such as haddock or sole
3	tablespoons lime juice
¹/2	teaspoon salt
3	tablespoons vegetable oil

Remove husks from tomatillos and wash peppers. Pour water 1/2-inch deep into a medium saucepan, than add fresh tomatillos. Bring to a boil, reduce heat, cover and cook 10 minutes or until tender. Drain and cool.

No need to cook canned tomatillos.

Place tomatillos, green onions, garlic, parsley and chile in blender or food processor and process until puréed. Heat 2 teaspoons oil in a medium saucepan. Add purée and salt to taste. Bring to a boil then reduce heat and simmer uncovered 15 minutes. Set sauce aside and keep warm. Sprinkle fish with lime juice and 1/2 teaspoon salt. Let stand 3 to 5 minutes. Heat 3 tablespoons oil in a large skillet. Add fish and cook 1 minute on each side. Add sauce then cover and simmer 5 minutes or until fish flakes easily when tested with a fork.

Serves 4-5

Bubba says . . .

"Drive 90, freeze a Yankee!"

Migas

4	eggs	1/4	cup chopped onion
1	tablespoon water	12-16	tortilla chips, broken into bite-sizes
1	tablespoon salsa		
1	tablespoon bacon drippings	1/2	cup grated sharp cheddar or portions Monterey Jack
1/4	cup chopped bell pepper		

Beat eggs lightly with water and salsa, then set bowl aside. In heavy skillet, warm bacon drippings over medium heat then add bell pepper and onion, sautéing until limp. Pour in eggs and stir as they cook. Add chips about one minute before eggs are done. Stir well. Remove from heat and add cheese. Stir and serve immediately with warm flour tortillas and salsa.

Serves 2

Sausage-Asparagus Bake

1/2	pound link sausages	1	(10-oz.) pkg. frozen asparagus
2	cups cooked rice	1/2	teaspoon salt
1	cup cottage cheese	1/4	teaspoon pepper
1/2	cup sour cream	1/4	cup fine bread crumbs
1/2	cup chopped red onion	2	tablespoons butter

Cook sausages over low heat until most of the fat has fried out, but do not brown. Drain and set aside. Mix rice, cottage cheese, sour cream and onion together. Cut the asparagus in bite-size pieces (reserving 4 spears to arrange on top) and stir into cheese mixture. Add salt and pepper and 1/2 the sausage cut in small pieces. Place remaining sausage on top. Pour into 9-inch shallow baking dish and sprinkle crumbs on top. Bake at 350° F. for 20 minutes, then place remaining asparagus on top. Return to oven and bake 10 minutes longer

Serves 4-6.

★

Broiled Cheddar and Egg Salad Buns

8   large hard-boiled eggs, chopped

2   cups sharp cheddar cheese, shredded

1   cup green bell pepper, chopped

3   tablespoons onion, grated

2/3 cup evaporated milk

3   tablespoons prepared mustard

1 1/2 teaspoon salt

1/4 teaspoon pepper

3   sandwich buns or rolls, split, buttered and toasted

Combine the eggs, cheddar, green pepper, onion, evaporated milk, mustard, salt and pepper. Spread each bun with about 1/4 cup of the egg mixture. Broil about 5 inches from the coils for 5 minutes or until cheese is melted. Serve hot.

Hot Turkey Sandwich

3   oz. turkey breast, roasted and sliced

1   slice toasted white bread

2   slices tomato

2   slices bacon, cooked and drained

SAUCE

2   oz. butter

3   oz. flour

3/4 cup cream

1/4 cup milk

1/2 cup grated Swiss cheese

Salt and white pepper to taste

Heat butter and add flour. Whisk and slowly cook for 5 minutes. Whisk in cream and milk then heat. Next, whisk in cheese until melted. Season and simmer for 30 minutes or until sauce is very think.

Quarter toast and place in an oven safe dish. Top with turkey and tomatoes. Cover well with sauce then bake at 400° F. for 10 minutes. Garnish with bacon.

★

Texas Style Quiche

6	slices bacon, fried and crumbled	1/3	teaspoon nutmeg	
4	eggs, beaten well	1/2	cup grated Cheddar	
1 1/4	cup milk (half & half is better)	2	cups grated Monterey Jack	
2	tablespoons flour	1	small can (4 oz.) chopped green chilies, drained	
1/2	teaspoon salt	1	medium onion, finely chopped	
1/3	teaspoon cayenne	1	unbaked 10-inch pie crust	

Whisk flour, eggs and millk. Add salt, cayenne and nutmeg and whisk in. Stir in all other ingredients.

Bake pie crust at 450° F. for 6 minutes. Lower oven to 350° F. Pour Quiche micture into pie crust and bake approximately 35 minutes or until set.

Saucy Pork Roast or Tenderloin

Rub into the roast

2	teaspoons garlic salt	1	teaspoon cracked pepper
1	teaspoon chili powder		

Bake 325° F. 1 hour. Pour the following sauce over the roast and continue to bake 45 minutes. Baste several times during baking and also when you serve it.

2	tablespoons vinegar	1/2	teaspoon chili powder
1/2	cup apple jelly	1/2	teaspoon garlic salt
1/2	cup ketchup		

Beat this together until it is smooth.

Chicken Italiano

4	boneless, skinless chicken breasts		4	cloves minced garlic
1	can cream of mushroom soup		1	teaspoon dried oregano
1	Pkg. onion soup mix		1	teaspoon dried basil
1	large can sliced mushrooms, with juice		1/2	teaspoon paprika
1	small can tomato sauce		1/2	teaspoon onion salt
1/3	cup white wine		1/3	teaspoon cracked pepper
			1/3	teaspoon salt

Place chicken in a sprayed pyrex dish about an inch apart. Mix all other ingredients together and pour over chicken. Bake 350° F. one hour.

Before serving, spoon sauce over chicken.

Bubba says . . .

"Most Bubbas and cowboys like their meat well done. They don't want their dinner leaving the table before they do."

Texas Tidbit

Remember the Alamo!

Texans do truly have true grit, not grits, but G-R-I-T! We're a hearty bunch because we are descended from a long line of gritty, hearty, strong people. When

I think of gutsy people I always remember the Alamo in San Antonio. Can you imagine knowing you're going to die just to slow down Santa Anna and his men and never having a chance to win the battle? If I had been there I'd have made a backdoor to the Alamo and there wouldn't be a Texas, but that's just me! I know I truly admire all the people who died there and all Texans do and always will. What courage they showed while under siege. We lost men like Davy Crockett, Bonham, Austin, Bowie and Travis and hundreds more men and women, some Texan, some not. These people showed true grit. Visit the Alamo if you haven't, its fascinating. I love the museum with the Bowie knife and Davy Crockett's coon skin cap along with the guns, clothing and memorabilia. You can go inside the structure and learn all about the siege, and you will always "Remember the Alamo."

★ *San Antonio is a fascinating city full of old world charm. In certain areas you could believe you are in Mexico. The Riverwalk is unique and a must while visiting San Antonio. It is close to the Alamo as are beautiful old hotels blending in with new upscale ones. There are lots of good restaurants also.*

"True Grits"
(And Other Side Dishes)

Best Beer Beans

1	lb. pinto beans, washed and picked	3	cloves garlic, minced
1	large diced onion	1/2	teaspoon chili powder
6	cups water	1	can beer
1	small can tomato sauce		Salt and pepper to taste

Put all ingredients, except for beer, in a large pot to simmer for 2 hours. Add beer and simmer another 2 hours.

Serves 4.

Black Beans Habañero Style

4	leeks, white part only, thinly sliced	1/2	cup chicken broth
2	cloves garlic, crushed	3	cups cooked black beans, drained
2	cups acorn or butternut squash, cubed	1/2	teaspoon dried thyme
1	Habañero, seeded, stem removed, chopped	1/2	teaspoon ground cumin
2	tablespoons olive oil	1/4	teaspoon ground black pepper
1/2	cup dry sherry	2	teaspoons red wine vinegar
		1	cup pine nuts

Use surgical gloves when you're handling habañeros.

Sauté leeks, garlic, squash and habañero in oil for 5 minutes. Add sherry and chicken broth; bring to a boil. Reduce heat and simmer, uncovered, about 30 minutes or until squash is tender. Add beans, thyme, cumin, black pepper and vinegar. Continue to simmer until beans are heated through. Stir in pine nuts and cook 1 minute longer.

Makes 6 to 8 servings, depending upon appetites.

★

Sassy Sour Cream Green Beans

2	tablespoons unsalted butter	3	tablespoons all-purpose flour
1	small onion, chopped	3/4	cup shredded cheddar cheese
1	lb. canned green beans, drained	3/4	cup breadcrumbs, mixed with 1/4 teaspoon cayenne
3/4	cup sour cream		

Preheat oven to 350° F. Melt 1 teaspoon butter in a heavy non-stick skillet on medium. Sauté onion 5 minutes, or until tender. Combine green beans and next 2 ingredients in a bowl. Salt and pepper to taste. Add sautéd onion and stir, then pour into a buttered casserole dish. Sprinkle with cheese. Melt remaining butter and stir into breadcrumbs. Sprinkle over casserole and bake 25 minutes.

Serves 4.

Mexican Green Beans

4	cans drained green beans	1	can cream of mushroom soup
1	can sliced water chestnuts, drained	1	small can onion rings
1	8 oz. jar Jalapeño Cheese Whiz		

Place green beans and water chestnuts in a 3 quart casserole dish. Heat together soup and Cheese Whiz until cheese melts. Pour cheese mixture over beans. Bake 30 minutes at 350° F. Spread onion rings evenly over the top and bake 5 minutes longer.

Serves 8-10 people.

Bubba says . . .

"Texans spell barbecue many ways - barbeque, barbecue, B-B-Q, Bar-B-Cue, Bar-B-Q, etc. Isn't that Amazing? So many different spellings for barbecue."

Sesame Green Beans

1	lb. green beans, trimmed and cut into 1/2-inch pieces	2	tablespoons soy sauce
2	tablespoons sesame seeds	2	teaspoons Oriental sesame oil
		1/8	teaspoon nutmeg

Place green beans in a steamer basket over boiling water, cover, and steam 8-10 minutes or until just tender. Heat a heavy non-stick skillet on medium and add sesame seeds. Shake skillet constantly until sesame seeds are golden., then reduce heat to medium low and stir in soy sauce, oil and nutmeg. Add green beans and toss.

Serves 4.

Baked Broccoli Casserole

This is great.

2	heads broccoli	2	tablespoons red bell pepper, chopped
1	lb. Velveeta cheese		
1/2	cups milk	1 1/2	cups Ritz Cracker crumbs
4	tablespoons onion, chopped	3	tablespoons butter or margarine

Preheat oven to 375° F. In a large saucepan, steam the broccoli until tender. In a small saucepan, melt the cheese on low heat, then add the milk, onion, and bell pepper. Stir until well blended. Layer the ingredients in a large casserole, beginning with the melted cheese, then adding the broccoli and sprinkling with cracker crumbs. Dot the crumb layer with butter and repeat. Sprinkle the final layer with additional cracker crumbs. Cover and bake for 20 minutes, then uncover the casserole and bake an additional 5 minutes, until crumb topping is lightly browned.

Serves 6.

★

Broccoli Dijon

1	lb. broccoli spears	1	stick butter
2	tablespoon fresh lemon juice	Salt and pepper to taste	
2	tablespoons Dijonnaise		

Steam broccoli until tender crisp. In small bowl cream butter then add mustard and lemon juice. Add mustard mixture to broccoli in pan and heat until melted. Season with salt and pepper to taste. Toss well and serve.

Serves 4.

Caramelized Carrots

12	large carrots	3	tablespoons orange juice
1 1/2	teaspoon salt	1/2	cup raisins (optional)
4	cups water	1	teaspoon cinnamon
1	cup honey	1/2	teaspoon nutmeg
1/4	cup brown sugar	3	tablespoons each oil and flour

Peel and cut carrots into small chunks, then boil until just tender. Add honey, brown sugar, orange juice, cinnamon, and nutmeg and cook on medium until the liquid begins to thicken and coat carrots. Add raisins and cook until the liquid is half evaporated. Place oil in frying pan and brown flour, then gradually add to the carrots to thicken. Stir mixture to remove lumps and cook slowly for another 5 minutes until done.

Serves 4-6.

★ *On January 10, 1901 "Spindletop" was "brought in" just 3 miles from Beaumont. It is Texas' most famous oil well. It is what started it all!*

Marinated Carrots

2	tablespoons parboiled sliced round carrots	1/4	cup oil
1	bell pepper, cut into thin strips	1	cup sugar
1	medium onion, cut into thin rings	1	tablespoon dry mustard
1	can tomato soup	3/4	cup vinegar
		1	teaspoon salt
		1/2	teaspoon small cracked pepper

Layer carrots, bell pepper and onion in a pyrex bowl. Bring remaining ingredients to a boil and pour over carrots. Cover and refrigerate overnight for full flavor.

Serves 6.

Sour Cream Noodles

1	8 oz. pkg. noodles	1	tablespoon melted butter
1/2	pint sour cream	1	teaspoon diced parsley
3/4	cup grated parmesan		

Cook noodles. Drain. Rinse all ingredients and pour into buttered casserole dish reserving one half the cheese. Bake 225° F. one hour. Sprinkle with remaining cheese.

Horseradish Sauce

3/4	cup mayonnaise	1/4	cup lemon juice
4	tablespoons horseradish	Salt and pepper	
1	tablespoon Worcestershire	1	teaspoon dried parsley

Whisk all ingredients together.

Good with beef or fish. Also good as a salad dressing.

Cilantro Carrots
(We use a lot of cilantro in Texas.)

2	lbs carrots, cut into 2 widthwise and quartered lengthwise	3	tablespoons olive oil
6	tablespoons water	2	tablespoons ground cumin
3	tablespoons fresh lemon juice	2	garlic cloves, pressed
		2	tablespoons cilantro, minced

Combine carrots and 6 tablespoons water in large saucepan, season with salt, then cover and boil 7 minutes or until carrots are just tender. Drain off excess water and transfer carrots to large shallow bowl. Mix in lemon juice, oil, cumin and garlic, then salt and pepper to taste. When cool, add cilantro.

Serves 6.

Baked Creamed Spinach

1	pkg. frozen, chopped spinach	4	oz. cream cheese
2	tablespoons onion, minced	1	tablespoon basil, chopped
1/2	teaspoon salt	3	tablespoons parsley
1/4	teaspoon pepper	2	hard boiled eggs, chopped
1/2	cup grated Monterey Jack		

Preheat the oven to 325° F. Place the spinach in 1/2 cup of boiling water, return to boil, then cover. Lower heat and simmer for about 4 minutes or until the spinach is broken up. Drain but do NOT press all the liquid from the spinach. Combine the spinach, salt, onion, pepper, cream cheese, basil, parsley and egg in a blender or food processor and process until just blended. Pour into a buttered 1 quart casserole. Bake for 30 minutes or until a knife inserted in the center comes out clean. Serve hot.

Serves 2-3.

Spinach Souffle

1	cup milk	1/8	teaspoon ground nutmeg
1 1/2	tablespoons cornstarch	1/2	cup chopped spinach
3	tablespoon chopped fresh marjoram	1/4	cup shredded Parmesan cheese
1	tablespoon instant minced onion	2	large egg yolks
		6	large egg whites
1/2	teaspoon pepper	1/4	teaspoon cream of tartar

Lightly coat interior of a 1-3/4-quart souffle or straight-sided baking dish with oil. In a 2- to 3-quart pan, stir milk smoothly into cornstarch. Add marjoram, onion, pepper, and nutmeg. Stir over high heat until mixture comes to a boil. Smoothly purée in a blender with spinach, 2 tablespoons Parmesan and egg yolks. In a large bowl, beat egg whites and cream of tartar on high speed until whites hold soft peaks. Fold spinach mixture into whites. Scrape into oiled dish. Sprinkle with remaining Parmesan cheese. With a knife tip, draw a circle on souffle top 1-inch from edge. Bake in a 375° F. oven 25 minutes or until richly browned and center jiggles only slightly when gently shaken.

Serves 2-3.

Oven-Fried Squash

2	lbs. zucchini and yellow squash	1/4	cup freshly grated bread-crumbs
1	teaspoon salt		
3	tablespoons melted margarine		Dried basil leaves
1/4	cup freshly grated Parmesan cheese		

Preheat oven to 350° F. Slice the squash thinly using a food processor. Toss the squash with the salt in a colander and set to drain for 2 hours. Lightly grease a large baking sheet and layer the squash slices, overlapping. Drizzle with melted margarine. Combine cheese and breadcrumbs. First, sprinkle cheese crumb mixture over squash, then sprinkle on basil and bake for 25 to 35 minutes until brown and crisp.

Serves 6-8.

★

Southern Fried Okra

(My daughter gave me this Texas recipe.)

1	lb. fresh okra, cut 1-inch pieces	2	eggs, beaten
1	large green tomato, diced	1/4	teaspoon salt
1	medium onion, chopped	1/4	teaspoon black pepper
1	clove garlic, minced (optional)	1/2	cup milk
1	jalapeño pepper, halved and sliced, remove seeds if too hot	1	cup cornmeal
		1/4	cup vegetable oil

Combine okra, tomato, onion, garlic and jalapeño in large bowl. In separate bowl combine eggs, salt, pepper, milk. Pour egg mixture over veggies and coat thoroughly. Gradually add cornmeal until mixture on the okra and at the bottom of the bowl are soaked up. Mix evenly until mixture is still gooey. Heat oil in 10 inch skillet. Reduce heat to medium-low. Cover and fry about 10-15 minutes or until underside is golden brown. Then invert on plate and slide other side up into skillet and cook uncovered 5-8 minutes until golden brown. Remove from skillet to paper towels to drain excess oil. Serve hot.

Serves 2-4.

Different Squash Dressing

2	lbs. yellow squash	1/2	cup celery, sautéed
1	pkg. cornbread mix	1	teaspoon poultry seasoning
1/2	cup onion, chopped and sautéed	Milk	
		1	tablespoon margarine

Preheat oven to 350° F. Bake cornbread according to directions. Add just enough milk to soften cornbread. Boil, drain and mash squash. Add onions and celery that has been sautéed in margarine and mix gently. Add pepper to taste. Bake 30 minutes or until golden brown.

Serves 6.

Steak Fries

(A real Texas side dish)

3	large baking potatoes, scrubbed and cut into 6 pieces each, lengthwise	1/4	teaspoon chili powder
		1/4	teaspoon garlic salt
		1/2	teaspoon cracked black pepper
1/4	cup oil		
1/4	teaspoon cumin	1/2	teaspoon salt

Mix the spices into the oil in a large bowl. Put the potatoes in the bowl and coat them well. Place potatoes on an ungreased baking pan as far apart as 1/2-inch. Do not layer. Bake at 400° F. until well browned and tender when tested. I always break one in two after about 30 minutes to test. Serve immediately.

Serves 4-6

German Fried Potatoes

So good!

4	potatoes, peeled and sliced	1/2	cup water
2	medium onions, peeled and sliced into rings	2	tablespoons oil
		Salt and pepper to taste	
1/4	cup margarine		

Heat margarine and oil in large heavy skillet. Add potatoes and make sure oil coats all pieces. Add onions and fry together about 15 minutes, stirring very carefully several times. Pour half the grease off potatoes. Pour water over potatoes and salt and pepper them at this point. Put a lid on. Reduce heat to low and cook about 20-25 minutes stirring carefully and occasionally.

★ I like to fry 3 or 4 pieces of bacon in skillet very crisp. Use this bacon grease instead of 2 tablespoons oil. Reserve bacon and crumble over potatoes later when done. This is one of my favorites.

Serves 5-6

Potato Casserole

A friend of mine makes this and I like it.

6-7	boiled potatoes (whole)	1	tablespoon chopped onions OR chives
1	pint sour cream	1/4	cup melted butter
1	can cream of chicken soup diluted with 1/4 cup of water		Salt and pepper to taste
1	cup shredded cheddar cheese		Corn flakes

Wash and boil potatoes until done, but not overdone. Cool, peel, then grate. Place in a buttered pan. Mix together sour cream, chicken soup, water, 1/2 cup cheese, onion or chives, and salt and pepper. Put on top of potatoes. Top with crushed corn flakes and melted butter. Sprinkle other 1/2 cup of cheese on top. Bake at 350° F. for 30 minutes.

Serves 8-10.

Red Cabbage and Potato Casserole

A Greek version of a German dish.

1	tablespoon olive oil	5	large potatoes (up to 6), boiled, mashed, and seasoned to taste
1	tablespoon butter		
2	large garlic cloves, finely chopped	2	cups medium cheddar cheese, shredded
1	small head red cabbage, thinly shredded	2	oz. feta cheese, crumbled
	Freshly ground pepper	1	tablespoon sweet paprika

Preheat oven to 350° F. In a large skillet, heat oil and butter. Add garlic and sauté. Add shredded cabbage and sauté until just wilted, not soft. Stir in lots of freshly ground pepper. Spread mashed potatoes in a lightly greased 9 x 12-inch baking dish. Cover with sauteed cabbage and cheddar cheese, then sprinkle with feta and top with paprika. Bake 20 to 25 minutes, until hot and cheese has melted.

Serves 6-8.

Potato Cakes

A good way to use leftover mashed potato.

2	cups mashed potatoes	1/8	teaspoon salt
1	egg white, slightly beaten		Pepper to taste
2	tablespoons chopped onion		1 teaspoon oil
2	tablespoons all-purpose flour		

In a medium sized bowl combine potatoes, egg white, onion, flour, salt and pepper. Meanwhile, heat oil in a large skillet on medium. When hot, put about 2 tablespoons potato mixture for each cake into skillet. Cook until well browned, then turn and brown other side. Keep cakes warm.

Serves 3-4.

Potatoes Au Gratin

2	pounds of potatoes, peeled and thinly sliced (about 5 cups)	1/4	teaspoon black pepper
2	tablespoons melted butter	1	cup grated cheddar cheese
1/2	teaspoon salt	1/4	cup fresh breadcrumbs

Preheat oven to 425° F. Lightly grease a shallow 1-1/2 quart casserole with butter. Arrange sliced potatoes in layers. Sprinkle with melted butter, salt and pepper. Top with grated cheddar cheese and breadcrumbs. Bake, covered, 30 minutes. Bake uncovered an additional 15 minutes or until potatoes are tender.

Serves 5-6

Bubba says . . .

"If you weren't born a Texan, just git here as soon as you can!"

Garlic Mashed Potatoes

4-5 garlic cloves, peeled	1/3 to 1/2 cup heavy cream
1 cup olive oil	1/4 cup grated American cheese
5 russet potatoes	2 tablespoons grated Parmesan
2 tablespoons butter	Salt and pepper to taste

Put the garlic and olive oil in a heavy saucepan over lowest possible heat and simmer 30-40 minutes or until soft. Drain off oil. Purée garlic and set aside. Meanwhile, prick potatoes with a fork and bake in at 400° F. for 1 hour, or until soft. While still hot, peel and mash. Melt butter in heavy cream, whisk in puréed garlic, then stir into potatoes. Stir in cheeses and season with salt and pepper. Spoon into a baking dish. Place in a 400° F. oven for 12 to 15 minutes, or until browned and bubbling.

Serves 8-10.

Texas Spanish Rice

1 cup long grain white rice	1/2 teaspoon salt
1 tablespoon vegetable oil	1 small can (5.5 fluid ozs.)
1/2 medium onion, chopped	stewed tomatoes
1 chicken bouillon cube	Water

Place 1 tablespoon oil in saucepan. Add rice and copped onion then sauté until rice is lightly toasted and onion softened. Add chicken bouillon cube and break it up with a fork. Salt to taste. Pour the small can of tomato juice into a two cup measuring cup and fill to the two cup mark with water. Pour the two cups of liquid into the pan with the rice mixture, cover and turn the heat down to low. Let cook on low for 20 minutes. When done, fluff with fork.

Serves 3-4.

★

Red Jalapeño Potatoes
Very good!

3	lbs. baking potatoes		$^{1}/_{3}$	cups pickled jalapeños, sliced plus 1 tablespoon pickled jalapeño juice
$1^{1}/_{2}$	tablespoon salt			
4	tablespoons unsalted butter			
4	tablespoons corn oil		2	tablespoons flour
1	medium green bell pepper, sliced		2	cups evaporated milk
			2	cups grated mild Cheddar cheese
3	garlic cloves, minced			
4	oz. pimentos, diced			

Place potatoes in large pan covered with at least one inch of water and add salt. Cook potatoes on medium 25-35 minutes or until tender. Drain and slice thinly. Preheat oven to 350° F. and grease large baking dish. Warm butter and oil in saucepan on medium. Add bell pepper, onions and garlic then sauté until softened. Stir in pimientos, jalapeños and jalapeño juice. Sprinkle with flour and mix. Gradually add milk and stir constantly. Simmer until thickened. Remove from heat, add cheese and stir well. Alternate layer of potatoes and sauce in dish, ending with sauce. Cover and bake 50 minutes 1 hour or until potatoes are soft.

Serves 8-12.

Broccoli Rice Casserole

(It's been around a long time for a reason)

3	pkgs. thawed chopped broccoli		2	cans cream of chicken soup
1	cup celery, chopped		2	cans cream of mushroom soup
1	large onion, finely chopped			
$^{1}/_{2}$	stick margarine		1	lb. Velveeta cheese
1	lb. sliced mushrooms		$^{1}/_{3}$	cup milk
2	cups uncooked rice		Salt and pepper to taste	
1	can water chestnuts			

Cook rice. Sauté veggies in margarine. Beat milk into soup. Cut cheese into cubes and melt into soups. Mix all together and bake at 375° F. 45 minutes.

Serves 8-12.

★

Louisiana-Texas Border Beans and Rice

2	cups dried red beans	3	bay leaves
Soaking water		2	teaspoons black pepper
3	quarts water	3	teaspoons cayenne
1	lb. smoked ham hocks	1/2	teaspoon salt
2	medium onions, chopped	6	tablespoons minced garlic
1	medium green bell pepper, chopped	Boiled rice	
2	ribs celery, chopped	Chopped parsley and scallions for garnish	

Cover the dried red beans with water and soak them overnight at room temperature. Pour off the water and place beans in a large, heavy pot. Add 3 quarts water and the ham hocks. Bring to a boil, lower heat, and simmer for 2 hours. Add the remaining ingredients, except rice and garnish, and simmer until the meat falls apart, about 2 more hours. Stir frequently and add more water if needed. Half an hour before serving, prepare the boiled rice. Serve the bean mixture over boiled rice and garnished with parsley and scallions.

Serves 3-5.

Chili Rice

2	cups rice	1/2	teaspoon cumin
1/3	cup margarine	1	can diced tomatoes (15 oz.)
2	teaspoons salt	2	teaspoons minced cilantro
1/4	teaspoon pepper	2	cloves minced garlic
1	teaspoon chili powder	1/4	cup finely chopped onion

Brown rice in margarine with garlic and onions. Add all the rest of the ingredients, plus enough boiling water to cover one inch above rice. Cover and simmer about 30 minutes.

Serves 5-6.

★

Chili Relleños

2	cans (4 oz. each) whole green chiles	3	tablespoons milk
1/2	lb. Cheddar cheese, grated	1/2	teaspoon salt
1/2	cup flour		Oil for frying
2	large eggs, beaten	2	can Rotel, heated

Stuff chiles with cheese. Coat generously with flour. Beat eggs and milk together. Dip chilies into egg mixture and back into flour. Repeat. Sprinkle with salt. Fry in hot oil until golden brown on both sides. Serve with heated Rotel.

Serves 4-6 people.

Corn Pudding

1	can whole kernel corn, drained	1/4	cup melted margarine
1	can cream corn	5	beaten eggs
1/2	cup flour	1/3	teaspoon cracked pepper
1	teaspoon onion salt	1	tablespoon dried parsley
1/4	cup sugar	2	tablespoons chopped pimento
		2	cups milk

Combine all ingredients and whisk well. Bake 375° F. until set.

Serves 6-8 people.

Bubba asked . . .

the "little woman" if she'd like to eat someplace she'd never been. Excitedly she answered, "Yes, I'd like to." So Bubba took her to the kitchen.

★

Asparagus Casserole

2   1 1/2 oz. cans drained asparagus
1 1/2   tablespoon butter
1   can cream of mushroom soup
1   4 oz. jar pimento, chopped
1   small jar Cheese Whiz
2   tablespoons milk

2   tablespoons grated onion
4   hard boiled eggs, sliced
2   cups cracker crumbs
1/3   teaspoon pepper
(Try this before using salt. I don't use salt as it has salty ingredients.)

Drain asparagus. Heat soup, Cheese Whiz, and milk together until cheese is melted. Melt butter in the bottom of a pyrex dish evenly and swish sides as well. Pour 1/2 of the soup mixture into the dish. Layer asparagus, onion, pimento and eggs. Pour the other half of the soup mixture over this and cover with cracker crumbs. Bake 350° F. 35 minutes.

Baked Sweet Onions Piquant

4   large sweet onions
1/4   cup unsalted butter
4   teaspoons Worcestershire sauce

2   teaspoons ground cumin
4   teaspoons brown sugar
1/2   cup chicken broth
1/2   cup dry white wine

Preheat oven to 425° F. With a sharp knife, cut out a 1-inch diameter by 3/4-inch-deep cavity in the top of each of the onions, reserving the scraps.

Sprinkle each onion with salt and pepper to taste and divide among the cavities the butter, Worcestershire sauce, cumin and brown sugar. Arrange the onions in a baking dish, add the broth, the wine and reserved onion scraps. Bake in a 425° F. oven, basting occasionally, for 45 or 50 minutes, or until golden and onions are very tender when pierced with a knife.

Fried Onion Rings

3	very large onions	2	eggs
Cold water		2/3	cup milk
1	cup flour	1	tablespoon oil
1	teaspoon salt	Oil for deep frying	

Peel the onions and cut into half-inch slices. Separate into rings. Put onion slices into a container of cold water and refrigerate for half hour. Drain well; batter will not adhere to wet onion rings.

Mix together flour and salt. Add the eggs, milk and tablespoon of oil, and beat until smooth.

With tongs, dip onion rings into batter, allowing excess to drip off. Deep fry in hot oil (375° F.), turning rings, until golden brown on each side, about 4 or 5 minutes. Be careful not to overcrowd your fryer. Drain on paper towels. Makes about 4 servings.

Pizza Sauce

1	6 oz. can tomato paste	1/4	teaspoon oregano
1	8 oz. can tomato sauce	1/4	teaspoon red pepper
2	cloves crushed garlic	1/4	teaspoon basil
1	teaspoon sugar	1/4	teaspoon salt

Combine all ingredients and mix well. Spread it on your pizza dough before adding your favorite toppings. (Add a little water if too thick.)

Cabbage Supreme

1	large head cabbage	1/2	teaspoon salt
1/4	cup margarine	1/3	teaspoon pepper
1/4	cup flour	2	cups milk

TOPPING

1/2	large onion, chopped	1/4	cup mayonnaise
1/2	cup chopped red bell pepper	3	tablespoons chili sauce
1 1/4	cup finely grated Cheddar cheese		

Cut cabbage into 8 wedges and steam about 10 minutes until tender, but crisp. Make a white sauce using the next five ingredients. Spread drained cabbage in a large pyrex dish. Pour white sauce over cabbage and bake 375° F. 20 minutes.

Mix topping ingredients together and spread over cabbage. Bake another 20 minutes.

Fried Cabbage

1	large head of cabbage, cup up	1	onion, finely chopped
6-8	pieces bacon		Salt and pepper to taste
1	can tomato sauce with tomato bits		

Fry bacon crisp, reserve grease. In bacon grease put cabbage and onion and fry stirring for 2 minutes. Pour tomato sauce over cabbage. Sprinkle with salt and pepper to taste.

Crush bacon over cabbage. Continue to cook on low, covered, 20 minutes.

Bubba says . . .
"Do you know why most Texans eyes are brown? Because they're full of it!"

★

Bubba's Irish Potatoes

14-16 medium Irish potatoes
2   cups sour cream
1/4 pound margarine
4   small green onions, finely chopped

12 slices bacon, fried and crumbled
2   cups grated Cheddar cheese
1   tablespoon dried parsley

Boil potatoes in their skins. Peel and cut into 1/2-inch cubes. Add margarine, sour cream, onions, half of the cheese and half of the bacon.

Mix well and place in buttered dish. Bake 350° F. for 30 minutes. Place the rest of the cheese on top of the potatoes and sprinkle the rest of the bacon and parsley on top. Bake another 8-10 minutes or until cheese melts and bubbles.

★ *Gruene Hall is Texas' oldest "honky-tonk." Gruene Hall is located in historic Gruene, Texas, just northeast of New Braunfels. A fun place!*

Ham and Macaroni Casserole

2	cups macaroni cooked in salt water	1/2	cup frozen green peas, thawed
2	cups cook ham, diced	3	cups cubed velveeta
1	egg	1	cup grated Cheddar
1/2	cup milk	1/4	teaspoon onion salt
2	tablespoons butter, soft	1/4	teaspoon pepper

Beat egg into milk, set aside.

Butter 9 x 9-inch pyrex dish and put cooked macaroni in it. Evenly distribute ham and peas on top of macaroni. Push cubes of velveeta down into the macaroni about 1-1/2 inches apart. Pour milk mixture evenly over the macaroni. Sprinkle with onion salt and pepper. Bake 325° F. one hour. Put grated Cheddar on top of casserole and bake until it melts.

My Best Aggie Joke

A highway patrolman was driving along a highway when he spotted an Aggie chasing a pig. The officer got out of his patrol car and asked "Why are you chasing that pig?" The Aggie answered "I'm afraid it might get run over on this busy highway." The officer asked "Where are you going to take the pig?" "I don't know," answered the Aggie. "Well," said the officer, "I'd take the pig to the zoo in San Antonio." "Good idea," responded the Aggie. The next weekend the same patrol officer was driving down the same highway and passed the Aggie with the pig in the cab of the pickup with him. He pulled him over and said, "I thought I told you to take that pig to San Antonio to the zoo." The Aggie answered, "You did and we enjoyed the zoo so much we're on our way to Six Flags this weekend."

Bierocks

(A really good German dish)

3	lbs. ground chuck
1	small head cabbage, shredded
1	small onion, finely chopped

Salt and pepper to taste

Favorite and easy bread dough (your own recipe)

2 eggs whites beaten with 2 tablespoons water

Fry ground meat with cabbage, onion, salt and pepper until done. Drain. Roll bread dough into squares. Place meat mixture in the center of bread square. Bring 4 corners together and pinch ends. Repeat. Place on a greased baking sheet at least two inches apart. Your dough should be about 1/4 inch thick. Put the pinched side of Bierock down on baking sheet. Let rise. Bake 350° F. for approximately 20 minutes. Brush with egg wash before baking.

Bubba says . . .

"Someone from another state asked Bubba if he wasn't a Texan what would he be? Bubba answered 'Ashamed.'"

Texas Tidbit

"Oh deer, oh dear"

Hunting is huge in Texas. We have deer hunters who wait with baited breath all year for "the season" to start. You see pickups galore with guns, deer blinds built on, and red caps. These make it easier for hunters to spot other hunters. The Texas restaurants and the meat processing plants are "abuzz" with deer hunters. Hunting is big business in Texas.

Many of our Texas deer hunters have hunting leases near the border so that they can have fun in Mexico, as well as hunt. Many of our deer hunters don't know the difference between deer and dear, however. Many have gotten into all kinds of trouble! But we'll never tell!

One of the funniest stories I've heard pertaining to Texas deer hunters goes as follows: Some very prominent Texans went down to their "close to the border" deer lease, got drunk in Mexico and enticed some women in the bar to come out to the deer lease and visit them one night. The young boy who operated the gate at the deer lease didn't speak English very well, and when told that their wives would be arriving on Friday and leaving on Saturday, and the women from the bar would visit on Sunday night, he got it slightly mixed up. When the wives arrived on Friday, the young boy excitedly ran out to meet the car and screamed, "Now you old whores go on back to Mexico. You're not expected until Sunday night. These men are expecting their wives today." This episode did a lot toward changing the hunting rules in Texas! Oh deer, oh dear!

★

Fair Game

(Anything you can hit with your bumper or shoot from your back yard.)

L.B.J. Ranch Deer Meat Sausage

I received this recipe from a friend who doesn't remember where she got it, but her husband loves it. I'm glad someone else is losing her memory. It yields 200 pounds.

1/2	deer	20	ozs. black pepper
1/2	hog	8	ozs. red pepper
25	ozs. salt	2	ozs. sage

Grind deer and hog and mix with remaining ingredients. Cook with scrambled eggs or form patties and pan fry.

You may freeze in freezer packs.

Hill Country Deer Jerky

4	lb. deer roast	1/4	cup whiskey
2	tablespoon Worcestershire sauce	1/2	teaspoon onion powder
1/4	cup salt	4	cloves garlic, minced
1/4	cup brown sugar	1	teaspoon ginger, grated
2	cups beer	2	teaspoons orange peel, grated
1	cup apple cider vinegar	1/4	teaspoon cayenne
1/3	cup soy sauce		

Trim fat from roast, cut into slices 1/4-inch thick by 1 to 2 inches wide. Place meat in marinade, made by combining above ingredients in glass bowl. Marinate for at least 24 to 48 hours in a cool place. Remove to wire rack and allow to air dry until glazed (about 45 minutes). Soak hickory chips in water and add to coals to smoke the jerky 12 to 14 hours at 150° F.

Country Venison Casserole

2	lb. ground venison	1	medium onion, chopped
10	slices of bacon	1	teaspoon garlic powder OR
2	cans of tomato soup		crushed garlic (optional)
2	cans of whole kernel corn, drained	1	pkg. chili seasoning
		1	box of cornbread mix

In a large skillet cook bacon. Remove bacon and drain on paper towel, save drippings. Brown hamburger and onions in drippings. Add the 2 cans of tomato soup and chili seasoning. Let simmer for ten minutes. After simmering layer the hamburger in a 9 x 14-inch baking dish. Then layer in the 2 cans of corn. Crush bacon and spread on top of corn. Mix cornbread batter (little runny), and spread on top of other ingredients. Bake at 350° F. oven until cornbread mix is golden brown.

San Marcos Venison Meatloaf

1	lb. ground venison	2	tablespoons parsley
1	8oz. can tomato sauce, undiluted	1	tablespoon Worcestershire sauce
1	cup Italian breadcrumbs	1/2	teaspoon salt
1	medium onion, chopped		Pinch rosemary springs
1/2	medium bell pepper, chopped	1	teaspoon garlic salt

Combine all ingredients and mix well. Press into 9 x 9 x 2-inch loaf pan. Cook in 350° F. degree oven for 25 to 30 minutes. Great served with mashed potatoes.

Serves 2.

Bubba says . . .

"Never walk behind the herd, any herd!"

★

Great Fried Deer Backstrap!

5	venison steaks cut 1-inch thick, backstrap is the best	1	cup all-purpose flour
			Salt and pepper
2	eggs		Seasoned salt
3/4	cup buttermilk	1/4	cup oil

Beat eggs and mix with buttermilk. Set aside. Mix all-purpose flour, salt, pepper, and seasoned salt. Dip steaks into buttermilk/egg mixture and then dredge them on both sides in the flour mixture. Fry for 7-10 minutes on medium-high heat until golden brown.

Serves 3-4.

Texas Venison Sausage

4	lb. ground venison	1/4	teaspoon nutmeg
4	lb. ground pork	1/4	teaspoon cloves
2	tablespoons salt	1/2	teaspoon All-spice
2	teaspoons black pepper	1/2	teaspoon garlic powder
1/2	teaspoon mace		

Mix venison and pork together. Add approximately 1/2 cup hot water to meat to gain desired texture for sausage press. Add spices and mix well.

Bubba says . . .

"If you love something, set it free. If it comes back to you it loves you and belongs to you. If not, hunt it down and kill it."

★

Duck a la'Orange

6	lb. duck, cut	1^1/$_2$	cup orange juice
^{1}/$_2$	cup red wine	1	tablespoon honey
1	tablespoon orange peelings	^{1}/$_4$	teaspoon ginger
2	cloves garlic, minced	^{1}/$_8$	teaspoon pepper
3	tablespoons oil	1	cup orange sections
1	tablespoon potato starch		

Puncture duckling generously with fork; place on rack in roasting pan. Pour most of the sweet red wine over duckling pieces. Roast in slow oven (325°F.), basting occasionally, allowing 25 minutes/pound. In medium saucepan, sauté orange peel and garlic in oil. Mix in potato starch until smooth. Slowly add orange juice, honey and remaining wine. Simmer 1 minute. Mix in ginger, pepper and orange sections; simmer 5 minutes. Serve hot sauce with roast duckling.

Serves 4-6.

Braised Wild Duck Breasts
in a Spiced Wine Sauce

8	duck breasts	1	cup corn kernels (frozen work well)
2	tablespoons olive oil		
2	large cloves garlic, crushed	^{1}/$_3$	cup Worcestershire sauce
1	cup chopped green peppers	^{1}/$_3$	cup red wine vinegar
2	cups sliced mushrooms		Salt and pepper
1	cup diced onion		Crushed oregano leaves
1	cup cubed potatoes		

Heat oil in wok until very hot. Add crushed garlic clove and let sizzle a minute or so. Add venison strips and sauté for a few minutes. Add potatoes and onions next and sauté for about 5 minutes, stirring every so often. Add Worcestershire sauce and red wine vinegar. Add salt, pepper and oregano leaves as needed to taste. Lastly, add green peppers, mushrooms and corn kernels, and cook only long enough that vegetables don't go limp. Tastes great with a topping of freshly grated Parmesan cheese.

Serves 4-6

Stuffed Quail

12	quail, dressed	1/4	cup all-purpose flour
1	lb. lean bulk pork sausage	2	cups red wine
12	slices bacon	2	tablespoons grape jelly
1/4	cup butter or margarine, divided	1/2	teaspoon salt
		1/4	teaspoon pepper

Rinse quail thoroughly with cold water; pat dry. Spoon sausage into body cavity of quail. Wrap 1 bacon slice around each quail, and secure with a wooden pick. Melt 1 tablespoon butter in skillet; add quail, 3 or 4 at a time. Cook until browned on both sides. Remove and place in a 13 x 19 x 2-inch baking dish. Repeat procedure with remaining quail. Drain pan drippings, reserving 1 tablespoon. Combine remaining 3 tablespoons butter and pan drippings in skillet; add flour, stirring until smooth. Cook 1 minute, stirring constantly. Gradually add wine; cook over medium heat, stirring constantly, until mixture is thickened and bubbly. Stir in jelly, salt, and pepper. Pour over quail. Bake at 325° F. for 45 minutes or until done.

Serves 4.

Bubba says . . .

He was hunting in the woods when he came upon a beautiful naked woman tanning on a rock. He asked, "Are you game?" She answered, "Yes, I am." So he shot her.

★

Baytown Green Peppercorn Duck

1	4-lb. duckling	1	bay leaf
2	tablespoons salt	2	teaspoons butter or margarine
2	quart water	2	teaspoons flour
1/2	cup chopped onion	1/2	teaspoons ground anise seed
1/2	cup chopped celery	1	tablespoon green peppercorns
2	garlic cloves, minced		in wine
Salt			

Remove backbone from duck and quarter or bone duck, reserving backbone and giblets for broth. Place salt in deep saucepan, add duck pieces and cook 20 minutes. Remove duck, place in shallow casserole and bake at 350° F. 45 minutes, increasing heat to 375° F. during last 10 minutes. Combine giblets, backbone and water in saucepan, cover and bring to boil. Reduce heat and simmer 2 hours. Skim off fat. Add onion, celery, garlic and bay leaf to broth, cover and simmer 20 minutes. Strain. Melt butter in saucepan, stir in flour and cook 1 to 2 minutes. Add broth and cook until slightly thickened. Add anise and green peppercorns and season to taste with salt. Serve sauce over duck.

Serves 4-6.

Wild Game Barbecue Sauce

1	bottle (14 oz.) ketchup	1	teaspoon mustard
2	tablespoons Worcestershire	2	teaspoons Tabasco
1	tablespoon lemon juice	3	cloves garlic, minced
1	stick melted butter	1/4	teaspoon chili powder
1/4	cup brown sugar	1/4	teaspoon cayenne
2	medium grated onions	1/4	teaspoon Liquid Smoke

Add all ingredients in a large sauce pan and simmer for an hour. Stir occasionally.

This keeps well in the refrigerator. It is great for basting wild meat. I also like it for chicken.

★

Texas Tidbit

Judge Roy Bean (1823-1903)

(the ONLY "Law West of the Pecos")

Judge Roy Bean was an unorthodox and uneducated judge who ruled from Langtry, Texas for some 20 years with controversy and an odd sense of humor. In 1882 Bean was appointed Justice of the Peace. He erected a shack that he both lived in and worked in. There were several signs outside, such as "The Jersey Lily," "Law West of the Pecos," "Justice of the Pecos," "Notary Public," and "Beer on Ice."

As Bean grew older he became more and more eccentric. The "Jersey Lily" was a combination courthouse and barroom, a real Texas western saloon. It was named the "Jersey Lily" for the actress Lily Langtry, as was the town. Judge Roy Bean was infatuated with Lily Langtry much of his life, but contrary to popular belief, they never even met. He had her pictures on the wall and was seen toasting her on a regular basis.

Judge Roy Bean was buried in Del Rio, Texas, unceremoniously. Oddly enough, Lily Langtry came to Langtry after his death to see the town named after her and visited the "Jersey Lily," taking away several momentos.

There are many Judge Roy Bean stories, but my favorite goes as follows. Bean found a dead body with a gun and $40.00 in gold on it. He fined the dead man $40.00 for carrying a gun and pocketed the money!

★

Judge Roy Bean was *Real Sweet* on Lily Langtree

George W.'s Statehouse Pecan Pie

A friend of mine gave me this recipe used by Laura and George W. Bush. She says it is George W.'s favorite. Let's compare it to LBJ's recipe! They are both excellent.

1¹/₂	cup Texas pecan halves	1	cup dark Karo
1	9-inch pie shell, unbaked	¹/₂	teaspoon vanilla
3	eggs	1	cup sugar
1	tablespoon butter, room temp.	1	tablespoon flour

Arrange pecans in pie shell and set aside. Beat eggs and add butter, Karo and vanilla. Stir. Fold in dry ingredients. Pour over pecans. Let sit until pecans rise to the surface. Bake 350° F. until set. Sounds real good to me!

Miriam ("Ma") Ferguson's Sugar Cakes (Cookies)

"Ma" Ferguson was the first woman governor of Texas. Much later Ann Richards was the second female governor of Texas.

1	lb. butter	1	teaspoon nutmeg
4	cups sugar	¹/₄	cup brandy
6	eggs	8	cups sifted flour
1	teaspoon salt	1	teaspoon baking powder

Cream butter and sugar. Add well beaten eggs, salt, nutmeg and brandy. Beat well. Sift flour and baking powder together. Add gradually to butter mixture until it forms a stiff dough. Put dough in covered bowl and refrigerate 2 hours. Remove and shape into small rolls. Cut and bake at 400° F. until slightly brown, 6 or 8 minutes only.

★

Fabulous Noodle Kugel

My cousin in Houston says this recipe is a favorite of the Barbara and George Bush family. Any favorite recipe of theirs is delicious I'm quite sure!

1 lb. wide egg noodles, cooked	3 cups milk
1 cup sugar	1 pint sour cream
1 lb. cottage cheese	1/2 cup melted butter
1 1/2 teaspoon vanilla	Cinnamon and salt to taste
1 cup white raisins	Cornflakes to top
7 beaten eggs	1/4 cup butter in small cubes

Mix all ingredients except corn flakes and cubed butter in large bowl. Pour into large buttered baking pan and refrigerate overnight. Put corn flakes on top and dot butter around. Bake in 350° F. preheated oven 1-1/2 hours.

Fudge Cookies

1 can sweetened condensed milk	1 cup plus 2 tablespoons sifted flour
1 12 oz. package chocolate chips	
2 tablespoons water	2 tablespoons vanilla

Melt chips, milk and water over hot water, add flour and vanilla and stir well. Drop by teaspoonsful on sprayed cookie sheet. Bake 325° F. 8 minutes.

Bubba says . . .

he wants to have his cake and eat it too! What else would he do with it, just sit around and look at it? Use it for a doorstop or maybe just carry it around all day? Hell yes, he'll eat his cake.

★

Pie Crust

6	cups sifted flour	1	beaten egg
1½	teaspoon salt	⅔	cup ice water
1	teaspoon baking powder	2	teaspoons vinegar
2½	cups shortening		

Sift flour, salt and baking powder together. Add shortening and cut in until crumbly. Add egg, water and vinegar. Pour over flour and shortening mixture and continue to "cut in" shortening until the size of peas. Form 4 equal balls. Chill before using. Use what you need and freeze the rest.

Texas Two Step
Chocolate Meringue Pie

3	egg yolks	1½	squares unsweetened baking chocolate
1	cup sugar		
1	tablespoon flour	1	cup milk
¼	teaspoon salt	1½	teaspoon vanilla
1	tablespoon butter		

MERINGUE

3	stiffly beaten egg whites	3	tablespoons sugar

Beat together until very stiff.

Beat yolks. Add sugar, flour and salt. Melt chocolate and butter together. Let cool and add to mixture. Add milk and vanilla. Mix well. Pour into unbaked pie shell. Bake 325° F. until set. Remove from oven and cover with meringue (all the way to sides). Bake until peaks are browned.

German Chocolate Cake

6	tablespoons sugar	1$^{1}/_{2}$	teaspoons vanilla
1$^{1}/_{4}$	cups cocoa	2$^{1}/_{2}$	cups flour
$^{3}/_{4}$	cups boiling water	$^{1}/_{4}$	teaspoon salt
1	cup butter	1	teaspoon soda
2	cups sugar	1	cup buttermilk
4	egg yolks	4	egg whites, stiffly beaten

ICING

2$^{1}/_{2}$	cups sugar	3	eggs, well beaten
2	cups evaporated milk	2	cups coconut
1	tablespoon flour	2	cups pecans, finely chopped
$^{1}/_{2}$	cup butter	1$^{1}/_{2}$	teaspoon vanilla

Combine 6 tablespoons sugar, cocoa and boiling water in saucepan. Cook until sugar is dissolved. Cool. Cream butter and 2 cups sugar until fluffy. Add egg yolks. Stir in vanilla and cocoa mixture. Sift flour, soda and salt and mix into sugar mixture alternately with buttermilk. Fold in egg whites. Pour into greased and floured 9-inch pans. Bake at 350° F. 30-35 minutes.

For icing mix all ingredients in saucepan and cook until sugar dissolves and becomes thickened. Cool.

Bubba says . . .
"Desserts is 'stressed' spelled backwards."

Cherry Cheesecake

1/4	teaspoon cinnamon	1	cup sugar
16	graham crackers	1	teaspoon vanilla
1/4	cup butter, melted	1	pint sour cream
2	tablespoons sugar	3	8 oz. packages of cream
4	eggs, separated		cheese

Preheat oven 350° F. Grease bottom of 9 x 3-inch spring form pan. Roll crackers. Take 3/4 of the rolled crackers and mix with melted butter, 2 tablespoons sugar and cinnamon. Press into bottom of pan. Beat egg whites stiff and set aside. In large bowl of mixer, combine cream cheese, yolks, 3/4 cup sugar and vanilla. Beat smooth. Fold in stiff egg whites. Place mixture in pan and bake about 50 minutes or until slightly brown. Remove from oven and pour the sour cream mixed with remaining 1/4 cup sugar over the top of cheesecake Return to oven for 10 minutes. Remove and cool. Sprinkle with crushed crackers. Chill overnight.

Cherry Topping

1	can sour cherries plus the juice	1/4	teaspoon cinnamon
1/2	cup sugar	1/2	teaspoon lemon juice
4	tablespoons cornstarch	1	tablespoon brandy

Whisk all ingredients except for cherries, but do use the juice. Boil and whisk until thick. Add cherries back and stir well. Chill until ready to serve.

Bubba says . . .

"Secede!"

★

Texas Praline Cake

1¹/₂   cups cake flour
1¹/₂   teaspoon baking powder
³/₄   cup sugar
¹/₄   cup shortening

¹/₄   teaspoon salt
²/₃   cup milk
1   egg
1   teaspoon vanilla

Sift flour, baking powder and salt together. Cream shortening, sugar and vanilla. Beat in egg. Add flour mixture alternately with milk, beating well after each addition. Pour into well sprayed glass baking dish. Bake 325° F. about 40 minutes or until done.

Icing

¹/₂   cup brown sugar
4   teaspoons flour
2   tablespoons water

4   tablespoons butter, room temperature
³/₄   cup pecans, chopped

Mix all ingredients together, carefully spread on top of cool cake. Return to oven and bake 10 minutes.

Cowboy Cookies

2¹/₄   cup shortening
2¹/₄   cup brown sugar
2¹/₄   cup sugar
1¹/₂   teaspoon vanilla
5   eggs
4¹/₂   cup flour

1¹/₈   teaspoons baking powder
2¹/₄   teaspoons baking soda
1¹/₈   teaspoons salt
4¹/₂   cups oats
12   oz. chocolate chips
1   cup chopped pecans

Cream shortening, sugars, vanilla and eggs. Stir together flour, baking powder, soda and salt. Mix all together. Add oats, chips and pecans. Drop onto sprayed cookie sheet with an ice cream scoop. Bake 350° F. 20 minutes or until edges start to brown.

★

Texas Ranger Cookies

I add a little cinnamon to these wonderful cookies.

CREAM

2	cups shortening		2	cups brown sugar
2	cups sugar			

ADD

3   eggs

STIR IN

4	cups flour		4	cups oatmeal (uncooked)
1/2	teaspoon cinnamon		4	cups Rice Krispies
2	teaspoons soda		1	cup coconut
1	teaspoon baking powder		1	tablespoon vanilla

Mix well and mold balls with your hands the size of walnuts. Put dough balls on a lightly sprayed cookie sheet and press down with your middle 3 fingers to 1/2 inch. Bake in a preheated 350° F. oven for 12-14 minutes.

"Better Than Sex" Cake

(Bubba's not sure he agrees)

1	18 1/2 oz. pkg yellow cake mix		1	6 oz. chocolate candy bar, broken up
1	3 oz. pkg. instant vanilla pudding		4	eggs
1/2	cup oil		1	cup chopped pecans
1/2	cup water		1	cup sour cream
1	6 oz. pkg chocolate chips			

Dump all ingredients in a bowl and mix well. Pour into a greased and floured 10-inch bundt pan. Bake 50 minutes in a preheated 350° F. oven.

Don't over-bake.

Mississippi Mud Cake

2	cups sugar	1/2	teaspoon salt
1	cup vegetable shortening	2	teaspoons vanilla
4	eggs	1	cup chopped nuts
1 1/2	cups flour	2	cups miniature marshmallows
1/3	cup cocoa		

Preheat oven to 325° F. Grease and flour 13 x 9 x 2-inch baking pan and set aside. Cream sugar and shortening with electric mixer in mixing bowl until light and fluffy. Add eggs, then beat on low until well blended. Combine flour, cocoa, and salt in separate bowl. Add to creamed mixture and blend well. Stir in vanilla and nuts. Pour into prepared pan and bake 35 to 40 minutes, or until toothpick inserted in center comes out clean. Remove from oven and sprinkle marshmallows evenly over top. Return to oven 10 minutes, or until marshmallows are melted. Cool in pan on rack. Frost with Mississippi Mud Icing. Chill before cutting into squares.

Mississippi Mud Icing

4 1/2	cup (16 oz.) powdered sugar	1/2	cup evaporated milk
1/3	cup cocoa	1	teaspoon vanilla
1	cup butter or margarine, melted	1/2	cup chopped nuts

Combine powdered sugar and cocoa in small mixing bowl. Add butter and blend well. Add milk and vanilla then beat with mixer until smooth. Stir in nuts.

Bubba says . . .

"If it ain't fried, it ain't mine."

Brandy Sauce
(for Pie or Gingerbread)

1	cup water	1/2	cup sugar
2	tablespoons cornstarch	1	teaspoon nutmeg
2	tablespoons butter, at room temperature	1/4	cup brandy
		1	teaspoon vanilla

In a small saucepan, mix the water, brandy, cornstarch and nutmeg. Bring to a boil and boil for 5 minutes. Remove from heat. Stir in the butter and vanilla. Serve hot over apple pie or gingerbread. Makes about 1 cup.

Applesauce Gingerbread

1	cup butter, melted	1	cup applesauce
1	cup brown sugar, firmly packed	2	cup all-purpose flour
1/2	cup molasses	2	teaspoons baking soda
2	large eggs	2	teaspoons ground ginger
		1	teaspoon ground cinnamon

Preheat oven to 350° F. Grease and flour a 9 x 13-inch baking dish. Combine melted butter, brown sugar and molasses in bowl. Add eggs, one at a time. Stir in applesauce and beat well. Sift the flour, baking soda, ginger and cinnamon into the batter. Mix thoroughly. Pour into the prepared baking dish, and bake for 35 minutes, or until a toothpick inserted in center comes out clean. Remove from oven and allow to cool for 5 minutes. Turn out onto a wire rack and cool completely.

Bubba says . . .
"You toucha my truck, I breaka your face!"

★

Apple Cake with Brown Sugar Icing

3   cups flour
1   teaspoon baking soda
1/2   teaspoon salt
1/2   teaspoon cinnamon
1/4   teaspoon allspice
1 1/2   cup oil
3   eggs
2 1/4   cups sugar

2   teaspoons vanilla
2   cup chopped pecans
3   cups chopped apples (peeled) OR one 20-oz. can of Comstock sliced apples (not apple pie filling), drained and diced

ICING:

1/2   cup butter
1/2   cup brown sugar, packed

1/4   cup milk

Preheat oven to 350° F. Grease and flour a 10-inch tube pan. Combine flour, baking soda and salt. Stir well, and set aside. Combine eggs, sugar and vanilla. Beat at medium speed for 3 minutes. Add dry ingredients at low speed. Batter will be thick. Add pecans and apples at low speed. Pour batter into prepared tube pan, and bake at 350° F. for 1 hour and 30 minutes, or until cake tester comes out clean when inserted in center of cake. Cool in pan for 10 minutes, then invert on serving plate and remove pan. Drizzle Brown Sugar Icing over warm cake

Brown Sugar Icing

1 1/2   cups evaporated milk
1 1/3   cups sugar
4   egg yolks, slightly beaten
3/4   cup butter

2   teaspoons vanilla
2   cups shredded coconut
1 1/2   cups chopped pecans

Combine the evaporated milk, sugar, egg yolks, butter and vanilla. Cook and stir over medium heat until thickened, about 12 to 15 minutes. Add coconut and chopped pecans. Cool until thick enough to spread, beating occasionally. Makes about 3 cups of frosting.

South Texas Pecan Pie

3	eggs, slightly beaten	1	teaspoon vanilla
1	cup sugar	1¼	cups pecans
1	cup Karo Light or Dark corn syrup	1	9-inch unbaked pie crust
2	tablespoons margarine or butter, melted		

Preheat oven to 350° F. In a large bowl, stir eggs, sugar, Karo and margarine until blended. Stir in pecans and pour into pie crust. Bake 50 to 55 minutes or until knife inserted halfway between center and edge comes out clean. Cool on wire rack.

Southern Pecan Praline Pie

½	cup sugar	1	tablespoon lemon juice
1	tablespoon flour	2	cups raisins
⅛	teaspoon salt	⅔	cup buttermilk
1	egg, beaten	1	unbaked 9-inch pie shell

Preheat oven to 425° F. Blend sugar, flour and salt. Add egg, lemon juice, raisins and buttermilk. Mix thoroughly and pour into pie shell. Top with following mixture.

Topping

½	cup firmly packed brown sugar	¼	cup butter, softened
⅓	cup flour	½	cup finely chopped pecans

Mix brown sugar with flour; cut in butter until crumbly. Add pecans. Sprinkle this topping over the filling that has been poured into the pie shell. Bake at 425° F. degrees for 15 minutes. Reduce heat to 350° F. and bake for an additional 25 to 30 minutes. Cool before serving.

Grasshopper Pie

1 1/4   cups chocolate wafer crumbs
1/3   cup melted butter
1   envelope unflavored gelatin
1/4   cup sugar
1/8   teaspoon salt
1/2   cup cold water

3   egg yolks
1/4   cup green creme de menthe
1/4   cup white creme de cocoa
3   egg whites
1/4   cup sugar
1   cup heavy cream, whipped

Combine crumbs and melted butter; press into 9-inch pie pan. Combine gelatin, sugar and salt in top of double boiler. Add water and egg yolks, one at a time, mixing well. Place over boiling water, stirring until gelatin is dissolved and mixture thickens slightly, about 5 minutes. Remove from heat, add creme de menthe and creme de cocoa. Chill, stirring occasionally until mixture is consistency of unbeaten egg whites. Beat egg whites until stiff but not dry, gradually add sugar, beating until very stiff. Fold egg whites into gelatin mixture, then fold in whipped cream. Pour into crumb crust. Refrigerate until serving time.

East Texas Sweet Potato Pie

6   cups cooked sweet potatoes, mashed
1 1/2   stick butter, melted
2   cups sugar
1/4   teaspoon cinnamon

6   large eggs, beaten
2   cups evaporated milk
3   teaspoons vanilla
1/2   teaspoons salt

Preheat oven to 350° F. Put mashed potatoes in bowl and add remaining ingredients (butter, sugar, eggs, milk, vanilla, cinnamon, salt) in order listed, then mix well. Pour in 9-inch unbaked pie crust and bake for 45 to 60 minutes.

Makes 3 or 4 pies.

LBJ Pecan Pie

This was supposedly his favorite pie.

1	cup sugar	3	eggs, beaten
1	cup corn syrup	1¹/₂	teaspoon vanilla
1	stick butter	1	8-inch unbaked pie shell
¹/₂	teaspoon salt		

Combine sugar, syrup, butter and salt. Cook until dissolved. Beat eggs until foamy. Mix together all ingredients and pour into pie shell. Bake 325° F. for 40 minutes.

Apple Crisp

6	cups diced apples		
1	cup flour	1	teaspoon baking powder
¹/₂	cup butter	1	teaspoon cinnamon
³/₄	cup sugar		Pinch of salt

Preheat oven to 350° F. Place 6 cups sliced apples in the bottom of a lightly greased baking dish. Cut in 1/2 cup butter to the remaining dry ingredients and crumble mixture over apple. Bake 30-40 minutes or until apples are tender.

Bubba says . . .

"A cowboy phoned home and told his wife he just broke his arm in two places. She answered, 'I thought I told you to stay outta those places.'"

★

Pick-a-Fruit Cobbler

1	stick margarine or butter
3/4	cup flour
1	heaping teaspoon baking powder
1	quart fruit (blueberries, peaches, apricots, blackberries, pear or apple) fresh or frozen
1/4	teaspoon cinnamon
1 1/2	cups sugar
1/2	teaspoon salt
2/3	cup milk

Melt butter in 2-quart baking dish. Combine dry ingredients, reserving 1/2 cup sugar. Stir into melted butter in baking dish. Add milk and stir again. Bring fruit and 1/2 cup sugar to boil. As soon as it boils, take off heat and pour over batter. Don't stir. Bake at 400° F. for 30 minutes.

Caramel Pie

3	eggs
3	tablespoons flour
1 1/4	cup white Karo
1/2	cup margarine
1 1/4	cup sugar
1	baked pie crust
1 1/2	teaspoon vanilla

Place all ingredients except vanilla and pie crust in a large skillet. Over medium heat, and stirring constantly, cook until mixture reaches a rolling boil. Continue to cook for 3 or 4 minutes beyond. It might stick, but that's OK. Add 1-1/2 teaspoons vanilla. Stir and pour into baked crust. Bake 350° F. for 25 minutes.

Bubba says . . .

"Welcome to Texas. Don't forget to go home."

Bread Pudding with Lemon Sauce

6	tablespoons margarine,	1/4	teaspoon salt, melted
12	slices thin white bread, no crust	2/3	cup sugar
1 3/4	cups plus 2 tablespoons milk	1/16	teaspoon almond extract
5	eggs, beaten	1	teaspoon vanilla
		3/4	cups raisins (optional)

Preheat oven to 375° F. Grease a 9 x 9-inch baking dish with 2 tablespoons melted margarine. Arrange bread and raisins (optional) in dish, higher on the sides than in the middle. Whisk remaining ingredients together and pour over bread, evenly soaking all pieces on top. Drizzle with remaining melted margerine and bake for 35-45 minutes or until it is fairly firm in center when shaken.

SAUCE

1	cup sugar	1	cup water
1/4	cup cornstarch	1/4	cup lemon juice
3	tablespoons margarine		

In large saucepan melt margarine. Whisk together sugar and cornstarch then add to saucepan. Add water to mixture and cook on medium until sauce boils and thickens. Stir constantly. Whisk in lemon juice and serve over pudding.

Bubba says . . .

"Never ask a man where he's from. If he's from Texas he'll tell you, and if he isn't there's no need to embarrass him!"

Mexican Sopaipilla

2	cups flour	1/2	cup buttermilk
2	teaspoons baking powder	1/2	cup water
1	teaspoon salt		Enough oil to fry
2	teaspoon oil		

Mix all ingredients (except the oil for frying) to form a dough. Roll 1/8 of an inch thick. Fold dough over and roll out again. Cut into 3-inch triangles. In hot oil in deep fryer drop dough and fry until golden. Drain well. Serve immediately with honey and powdered sugar.

Vanilla Custard

6	eggs	4	cups milk
1	cup sugar	1 1/4	teaspoon vanilla
1/4	teaspoon salt		

Scald milk and set aside. Butter 8 custard cups. Beat eggs, sugar and salt in a mixer for 3 minutes. Slowly add scalded milk on low speed. Add vanilla. Place custard cups in a pan that has 2 cups HOT water in it. Bake in preheated 425° F. oven for 10 minutes. Reduce heat to 325° F. and bake 40 minutes more.

Serve hot or cold

Bubba is . . .

"The definition of gross ignorance is still Bubba and 143 of his relatives and friends."

Pumpkin Flan

1/3	cup sugar	1	teaspoon ground cinnamon
5	eggs	1	teaspoon vanilla
3/4	cup sugar	1	cup pumpkin purée (canned or fresh cooked)
1/4	teaspoon salt		
1/3	cup water	1 1/2	cup whole milk

Make a hot water bath for the flan by setting a 9 x 1-1/4-inch-deep pie or cake pan in a larger pan. While holding down metal pie or cake pan so it won't float, fill outer pan with just enough hot water to come up around the smaller pan. Then remove the smaller pan and put the larger pan of water in a preheated 350° F. oven while you mix the flan.

Melt the 1/3 cup sugar directly in the pie or cake pan the flan will be baked in. To melt evenly, hold the pan securely (wear a good oven mitt or use tongs) over or just resting on a burner; shake and tilt the pan, rather than stirring the sugar. Watch carefully. Once melted, sugar will caramelize and brown quickly; as soon as it does, tilt pan so that the entire surface is covered. Remove from heat; syrup will harden and crack, but that's okay.

Beat together eggs and the 3/4 cups sugar; add the salt, water, cinnamon, vanilla, pumpkin and milk. Set caramel-lined pan in hot water in oven; pour in egg mixture carefully. Bake in a 350° F. oven for about 25 minutes; test doneness by gently pushing custard in center with back of a spoon – when done a crevice about 3/8-inch deep forms.

Remove from hot water and chill at once. (as the flan cools, the caramel dissolves.) When cold, loosen custard edge with a knife, then cover with a rimmed serving plate. Holding plate in place, quickly invert. The flan will slowly slip free and the caramel sauce flow out. To serve, cut in wedges, spoon on sauce.

Makes about 8 servings.

Stacy's Brownies

4	eggs	1 1/2	cup flour
1	cup oil	1	teaspoon salt
2	tablespoons Karo	1	teaspoon baking powder
2	cups sugar	1	tablespoon bourbon
6	tablespoons cocoa	1	cup chopped pecans
2	teaspoons vanilla		

In a large bowl, mix toether sugar, oil, bourbon, cocoa, vanilla and Karo. Add eggs and stir only until eggs barely disappear. Add the rest of the ingredients and mix only until flour disappears. Bake in a greased 9 x 9-inch pan for approximately 40-45 minutes.

Lisa's Cream Cheese Brownies

Use Stacy's brownie mix and after pouring mixture in the pan make the cream cheese mixture below.

Whip together:

1	8 oz. pkg cream cheese, soft	1	egg
1/4	cup sugar	2	tablespoons milk
1	teaspoon vanilla	1/4	cup flour

I Make four "logs" down the pan with the cream cheese mixture. Use a long pronged fork and make 3-inch swirls along the logs which in turn mixes the brownie and cream cheese mixture together making swirls. Bake 350° F. approximately 50 minutes.

★ My secret to taking brownies out when they are barely done is when they start to "fall" about half way across the pan.

Texas Chewy Pecan Pralines

1	cup sugar	3	cups pecans
1	cup brown sugar	1/2	teaspoon almond extract
1	cup Karo	1 1/2	teaspoon vanilla
1/2	lb. butter		
1	can sweetened condensed milk		

Combine sugars, Karo, butter and milk. Stir over medium heat, stirring constantly until it forms a soft ball when dropped into a cup of cold tap water. Remove from heat and add pecans and flavorings. Stir until thick. Drop by spoonsful onto a buttered piece of waxed paper.

Easy Strawberry Jello Salad

1	large box strawberry jello	1	large Cool Whip
1	10 oz. carton frozen strawberries, thawed and drained, but cold	1	cup small curd cottage cheese

Put all ingredients in a large metal bowl and fold together until jello mixture disappears. Do not overmix. Pour into a dish and refrigerate until serving time.

Isn't this easy? I served it at the Texas Tea Room for many years.

When strawberries are in season I add extra fresh strawberries to the recipe.

Bubba says . . .
"If you haven't been in Texas for 50 years, you're a newcomer!"

★

Stacy's Luscious Lemon Bars

This recipe is done in 3 easy stages.

CRUST:

2	cups flour	1	cup softened butter or
1/2	cup powdered sugar		margarine

FILLING:

4	eggs	1	teaspoon baking powder
2	cups sugar	1/3	cup lemon juice
1/4	cup flour		

GLAZE:

1	cup powdered sugar	3 1/2	tablespoon lemon juice

Preheat oven to 350° F. Combine crust ingredients and mix on low until crumbly. Put into a sprayed 9 x 13-inch pan. Bake 20-25 minutes or until lightly browned. Cool until warm.

Combine filling ingredients (except lemon juice) in a large bowl. Add lemon juice, stir well. Pour filling mixture over warm crust and bake 25-30 minutes. Cool completely.

Combine glaze ingredients, mix well until smooth and drizzle over top evenly. Let set well. Cut into bars.

Cowboys say . . .
"The strongest thing in the world is campfire coffee."

Mile High Strawberry Pie

1/2	cup whipping cream	3/4	cups sugar
2	tablespoons sugar	1/4	teaspoon salt
1	10-oz. pkg. frozen strawberries	1/2	tablespoon lemon juice
2	egg whites	1	teaspoon vanilla

In small mixing bowl beat whipping cream until stiff, adding 2 tablespoons sugar gradually as it beats. Place in the refrigerator in another bowl.

Wash bowl and beaters in cold water and dry to use again. Now beat together: package of strawberries, egg whites, sugar, salt and lemon juice. Add the sugar slowly while beating. Beat on high for 15 minutes. Add the vanilla at the end. Fold the two mixtures together very gently. Pour into a baked pie crust or into a baked graham cracker crust. Place in the freezer uncovered.

Serve frozen.

Garnish with whole strawberries all over the top, tips up. This is a great dessert to do ahead and forget about it until serving time. Everyone loves it and it looks like you slaved all day!

Praline Meringue Kisses

1	egg white, very stiffly beaten	1	tablespoon flour
		1	teaspoon vanilla
1	cup brown sugar	2	cups chopped pecans
1/2	teaspoon salt		

Mix all ingredients together and drop onto well sprayed cookie sheet.

Bake 15 minutes at 275° F. or until cookies start to brown.

Dr. Pepper Cake & Frosting

Texans are big on Dr. Pepper!

2	cups sifted all-purpose flour	1/2	cup shortening
1 1/2	teaspoon baking soda	2/3	cup buttermilk
1	teaspoon salt	2/3	cup Dr. Pepper
1 1/3	cups sugar	1	egg
1/2	cup cocoa	2	egg yolks

Preheat oven to 350° F. Grease and flour two 9-inch pans. Into large electric mixer bowl, sift together the sifted flour, baking soda, salt, sugar and cocoa. At low speed, add the shortening, buttermilk and Dr. Pepper, and mix 2 minutes, scraping sides of bowl as needed. Add the egg and egg yolks, and continue to beat for 2 minutes.

Pour batter into prepared pans. Bake at 350° F. for 30 to 35 minutes, or until cake tester comes out clean. Cool and frost with Dr. Pepper Frosting.

Dr. Pepper Frosting

2	egg whites	1/3	cup Dr. Pepper
3/4	cup sugar	1/4	teaspoon salt
1/3	cup light Karo syrup	1/4	teaspoon cream of tartar

Combine all ingredients in top of double boiler. Cook over rapidly boiling water, beating continuously with a portable electric mixer, until mixture stands in peaks. Remove from heat, and continue beating until thick enough for spreading.

Bubba says . . .

"The other white meat is cat."

Kahlua Devil's Food Cake

3	eggs, separated	$2^1/4$	cup all-purpose flour
$3/4$	cup sugar	$1/2$	cup cocoa
$1/2$	cup butter	$1^1/2$	teaspoon baking powder
1	cup light brown sugar, packed	$3/4$	cup strong cold coffee
		$3/4$	cup Kahlua

Preheat oven to 350° F. Grease and flour two 9-inch pans. Beat egg whites until frothy, then beat in sugar until stiff peaks form. Set aside. Cream butter and brown sugar together letting electric mixer run for about 5 minutes. Beat in the egg yolks one at a time. Sift the flour, cocoa and soda together. Add to creamed mixture alternately with coffee and liqueur; blend well. Fold egg whites into batter. Pour into prepared pans. Bake at 350° F. 30 to 35 minutes or until a cake tester comes out clean. Cool 10 minutes, invert on a wire rack and remove pans. Allow to cool completely before frosting.

Kahlua Chocolate Frosting

6	tablespoons butter	3	tablespoons Kahlua
1	lb. sifted confectioner's sugar	2-3	tablespoons hot coffee
3	tablespoons cocoa		

Cream together the butter and sugar. Beat in the cocoa, coffee and liqueur. Beat until smooth.

★ *The famous Texas Rangers were formed in 1835 by Stephen F. Austin. The Rangers were originally formed to protect settlers from hostile Indians. This small group of men became legendary taking on outlaws, bandits and all manner of dangerous tasks. There have never been any more courageous men than the Texas Rangers.*

★

My Peach Cobbler

8	cups sliced peaches (fresh peaches)	1/8	teaspoon nutmeg
1/3	cup flour	1	cup water
2	cups sugar	1/2	cup melted butter
3/4	teaspoon cinnamon	1/8	teaspoon salt

Mix flour, sugar, cinnamon, nutmeg, and salt together. Mix well. Stir in peaches.

Prepare cobbler dough and add peach filling. Bake 350° F. 1 hour. You can use canned sliced peaches with the juice and omit the water, if desired.

CRUST

3	cups flour	1	teaspoon cream of tartar
2	teaspoons baking powder	3/4	cup butter, melted
3	teaspoons salt	1	cup milk
3	tablespoons sugar	1	beaten egg

Combine all dry ingredients in large bowl. Mix in butter, milk and egg. Mix thoroughly. Roll out 2/3 of the dough on a floured board approximately 1/3-inch thick. Place in a 9 x 13-inch baking dish and add prepared fruit. Roll out the other 1/3 of dough and place over fruit, fluting the edges to seal. Cut slits in the top crust. Put a small bit of butter in the slits. Sprinkle top with sugar.

Bubba says . . .

"Hop Scotch reminds him of an amateur walking through a pasture full of cow patties."

Apple Dumplings

PASTRY

$2^1/4$	cups flour	$3/4$	cup shortening
$3/4$	teaspoon salt	8	tablespoons water

FILLING

6	medium apples	$1^1/2$	teaspoon cinnamon
$2/3$	cup sugar	$1/2$	tablespoon butter for each apple

SYRUP

1	cup sugar	4	tablespoons butter
1	teaspoon cinnamon	2	cups water

Mix and roll out dough 1/8-inch thick on floured board. Cut i 7 -inch squares. Core apples and fill cavity with sugar mixture. Dot with butter. Place apples on squares and moisten points of squares. Bring ends up over apples and overlap them, sealing them together very well. Place 2 inches apart in a 9 x 13-inch pan and chill.

Heat syrup ingredients. Boil 2 minutes. Pour hot syrup over dumplings. Bake 450° F. until slightly brown. Lower oven temperature to 350° F. and bake 35-40 minutes.

To serve place in the center of a dessert plate and spoon syrup over. Serve very warm. A scoop of ice cream is good with this. Spoon syrup over ice cream also.

Bubba says . . .

"My kid can beat up your honor student."

Raspberry Oatbran Bars

1/4	teaspoon salt	3/4	cup butter
1	cup flour	1	12-oz. jar raspberry
1	cup quick oats		preserves
1/2	cup oat bran	1	tablespoon vanilla
1/2	cup brown sugar	1/4	cup honey
2/3	cup cinnamon		

In mixer cream sugars with butter for 5 minutes on medium. Add salt, cinnamon, flour, oats, oat bran, honey and vanilla. Blend on low only until mixed well. Don't over mix as it will pulverize the oats. Place 1/2 of the oat mixture in a sprayed 9 x 9-inch baking pan. Spread the preserves over the oat mixture. Sprinkle the other half of the oat mixture over and spread evenly, gently pressing down.

Bake 350° F. 30 to 40 minutes or until lightly brown. Let cool completely before cutting into bars.

Graham Cracker Crust

1 1/4	cup graham cracker crumbs	6	tablespoons melted butter
1/4	cup sugar		

Mix and press into a 9-inch pie tin. Bake 375° F. approximately 6 minutes.

Chocolate Chip Pecan Pie

Use your favorite pecan pie recipe. Delete half of the butter called for and add 5 ounces chocolate chips to the recipe. Cool completely before slicing.

★

Texas Tidbit

We Texans drink as much as we eat. Beer is consumed in large quantities, although Texans are not all a bunch of drunks, don't you know? Texans drink beer with certain foods such as barbecue, burgers and Mexican food. Margaritas are plentiful at Mexican restaurants also. We don't tend to drink beer as much at Chinese or Italian restaurants. The more affluent Texans, while probably beer drinkers, are generally wine connoisseurs as well. Texas is into producing some very good wines. Be on the look out for them. Texans usually do things right!

"Watering holes" have started to change somewhat in Texas. For years such places as Gilley's in Houston (or Pasadena, I believe) and Billy Bob's in Ft. Worth were the rage. If you haven't seen the movie "Urban Cowboy," rent it and enjoy a glimpse into the Texas lifestyle of the young blue collar workers in Texas. It's a good movie and indicative of Texas; the way it was, the way it is, the way it always will be. At Gilley's and Billy Bob's you see acres of dance floors, souvenir shops, bull riding, stetsons, boots, denim and anything else that is representative attire of Texas, in spades! Billy Bob's enjoyed the distinction of being the world's largest honky tonk and Gilley's not far behind. However, I perceive a change to a smaller more intimate climate in the joints coming on. In Texas that could still mean 6 or 8 thousand square feet! We have trouble doing anything small in Texas. It might ruin our "big, big" reputation. Whether the dance hall is huge or small, Texans will still be dancing across Texas seven nights a week and having a few beers. Bottoms up! Long live longnecks and God bless Texas.

Ice houses are prevalent all over Texas and converted into all manner of "watering holes." I do not claim that they are unique to Texas but I have not noticed them in other states. Even the name Ice House is widely used in Texas even though the building wasn't originally an ice house. Two good examples in Austin are Waterloo Ice House featuring great burgers, and Bubba's Ice House gets two thumbs up for authentic, really good Texas fare. The decor is true Bubba.

Beverages

Hey, It's Texas!

Beer

Iced Tea

Dr. Pepper

Texas Tidbit

Texas Legacies

There is a lot to be "passed down" in Texas. Pride of family and love of state and country are just a few of them. We pass down our heirlooms and even lesser things. Whether you're rich or poor in Texas, the recipes that are passed down from generation to generation don't cost a dime, but are beyond treasure

I'm afraid we're getting away from that tradition somewhat. I see it all around me. I am inundating my daughters with recipes my family has used forever. I hope they not only use them, but pass them down to their children and so on. I know they'll add some recipes of their own to be enjoyed and passed down also.

Most of my recipes are steeped in Texas tradition. It is common to see Poteet strawberries, Stonewall peaches and other Texas towns listed on my recipes. I believe these places have superior products for the nation, not only Texas. The strawberries and peaches are smaller in size, but they're giants in flavor. The Rio Grande Valley grows wonderful produce. No one has a better grapefruit than the Ruby Red! Luling produces full flavored watermelons. Maybe these are the reasons Texas produces such good crops, we have so much to work with. God bless Texas!

Crowd-Pleasing Breakfast Tacos

(Makes about 30)

2	lbs. ground sausage	1/3	cup milk
1/2	teaspoon onion salt		Salt and pepper to taste
1/2	teaspoon garlic salt	2/3	cup salsa (medium)
1	teaspoon chili powder		Potato casserole (recipe below)
36	large eggs		

Sauté first 4 ingredients together until sausage is done, then drain on paper towels, reserving grease in pan. Add eggs to grease and stir in milk then cook until done, but not over cooked. Salt and pepper eggs to taste. Combine eggs and sausage then add salsa, but don't stir. Add hash brown casserole and gently stir.

Serve with flour tortillas.

Hash Brown Casserole

(to be added to Breakfast Casserole Filling)

1	stick margarine, melted	1/2	teaspoon onion powder
2	lbs. frozen hash browns	1/2	teaspoon garlic salt
1	cup milk		Salt and pepper to taste

Preheat oven to 400° F. Place melted margarine in bottom of 9 x 9-inch baking dish. Put hash browns in dish and mix together remaining ingredients in a small bowl, then pour over hash browns. Bake for 1 hour or until tender.

This recipe can be downsized easily.

Cowboys say . . .
"It's so much easier to walk with a horse underneath you."

Texas Tortilla Soup

6	chicken breasts	1/4	cup chili powder
4	quarts chicken broth	1/4	cup cumin
3	cups chopped yellow onion	1/4	cup garlic powder
3	cans Rotel		Salt and pepper to taste
3	tablespoons minced cilantro		

GARNISH WITH:

Shredded Monterey Jack cheese	Tortilla chips
Sour cream	Sliced avocado
Green onion, chopped finely	Lime wedge

Simmer chicken an hour. Drop chicken in boiling water 1-inch above it in the pot. Add Rotel, onions, chili powder, cumin, garlic powder and cilantro. Simmer another hour. Pull chicken into bite-sized pieces. In each bowl ladle 1 cup of soup onto crumbled tortilla chips. Garnish.

Serves 8-12.

Cowpoke Pintos

3	cups dried beans	1 1/2	teaspoon salt
6	bacon slices, cut up	1/3	teaspoon pepper
1/3	teaspoon onion powder	1/3	teaspoon sugar
1/3	teaspoon chili powder		Water to cover beans 2-inches
1/4	teaspoon cumin		above bean line (add 1/4 teaspoon cayenne for hot beans!)

Wash and sort beans. Cover with clean water and simmer for several hours with bacon. Stir and check water level several times throughout this process. Add boiling water when necessary. After 1-1/2 to 2 hours add all seasonings and continue to cook, uncovered, until desired thickness. Stir often when you uncover pot.

Serves 4-8.

★

Not So Plain Potato Salad

Everyone has their favorite potato salad. This is my favorite.

4	potatoes	1	tablespoon grated onion
1	cup mayonnaise	1	teaspoon vinegar
1	tablespoon mustard	1/2	teaspoon salt
1/4	cup sweet pickle relish	1/2	teaspoon small cracked pepper
1/4	cup dill pickle relish	2	teaspoons margarine
1/2	cup chopped celery OR	1/4	teaspoon paprika
	1/4 teaspoons celery seed	4	hard boiled eggs, sliced
			Pinch dried parsley

Boil potatoes, peel and cube into 3/4-inch cubes when cool. Place potatoes in large bowl and add: pickle relishes, onion and celery. In a sauce pan place margarine and heat on low until margarine melts. Remove from heat and stir in celery seed, mayonnaise, mustard, vinegar, salt, pepper and paprika. Whip together and pour onto potato bowl. Toss the potatoes and dressing taking care not to mash the potatoes. I garnish my potato salad bowl with boiled egg wedges and sprinkle a pinch of dried parsley. Serves 6-8.

Brazos Valley Baked Beans

2	14-oz. cans baked pork & beans	1	teaspoon mustard
1/2	cup packed brown sugar	1	small finely chopped onion
1 1/2	cup ketchup	2	tablespoons molasses
1/3	cup water (sloshed around in the bean can)	4	slices bacon
		1/4	teaspoon each salt and pepper

Fry bacon strips half way done. Reserve bacon. Pour bacon grease into a pyrex dish you're using to bake the beans. Swish it around on bottom and up the sides with a paper towel. In the pan you fried the bacon in sauté your onion clear. Put beans, brown sugar, ketchup, water, mustard, sautéed onion, molasses, and salt and pepper in a large bowl. Mix well and pour into the pyrex dish you greased. Add the bacon strips across the top of the beans. Bake 1 hour at 375° F.

★ One of my favorite meals is to make these beans and then place about 6 thin pork cops on top and bake this way. Turn chops over half way through baking. Salt and pepper the chops when you turn them. You can also use sausage links in this dish.

Serves 4-6.

Diane's "Braggin' Rights" Chili

4¹/₂ lbs. ground chuck
5 large cloves garlic, finely
4 pieces bacon, save grease

2 large onions, finely chopped
1 large bell pepper, finely chopped

Sauté the above in saved bacon grease (you can use 1-1/2 tablespoons oil if preferred. Drain well.

ADD:
¹/₂ cup chili powder
¹/₂ tablespoon ground cumin
1 teaspoon paprika
1 teaspoon salt
¹/₄ teaspoon pepper
1 teaspoon cayenne pepper
   (1¹/₂ teaspoons for hot, hot
   2 teaspoons, if you want to cry)

8 bouillon cubes
1 15-oz. can diced tomatoes
1 6-ox can tomato paste
4 15-oz. cans water
2¹/₂ tablespoons flour
Crush bacon slices and add to pot

Simmer everything but the flour very slowly for 2 hours. Then whisk 2-1/2 tablespoons flour into 1 cup of water and add to the chili stirring very well until it simmers again. Simmer 20 minutes stirring occasionally.

Serves a small crowd.

★

Beef Fajitas

2   skirt steaks, 1to 1¹/4 lb. each

MARINADE

1	Cup red wine vinegar	3	jalapeños, minced
¹/2	cup Tequila	1	tablespoon Worcestershire sauce
¹/4	cup oil		
	Juice of 3 limes	2	tablespoons black pepper
4	garlic cloves, minced	1	teaspoon dried oregano
3	tablespoons dark brown sugar	1	teaspoon cumin seeds, ground
			Salt to taste

Cut steaks diagonally across the grain into strips about 1/2-inch thick. Place meat in dish. Combine all marinade ingredients in bowl, mix well, and pour over meat. Refrigerate, covered, for 24 hours. Drain meat then fry them for 1-2 minutes in a heavy skillet. Serve with warm flour tortillas, onions, pico de gallo or salsa, guacamole and cheese.

Serves 4-6.

Bubba says . . .

"Advice is like a bowl of Texas chili. You should try a little before giving anyone else any!"

Chicken Fried Steak

1³/₄- 2 lbs. round steak, sliced
    1/2-inch thick and twice
    tenderized by butcher
2   cups flour
2   teaspoon baking powder
1   teaspoon baking soda
1   teaspoon black pepper

³/₄   teaspoon salt
1¹/₂   cup buttermilk
1   egg
1   tablespoon Tabasco
2   cloves garlic, minced
Vegetable shortening for frying

Cut steak into 4 equal portions and pound until 1/4-inch thick. Place flour in a shallow bowl and stir together baking powder and soda, pepper, salt, buttermilk, egg, Tabasco and garlic in a second bowl. Dip each steak first in flour, then in batter, then back in flour until the meat's surface is dry. Put enough shortening in a cast-iron skillet to create 4-inch of fat, then bring the temperature up to 325° F. Fry steaks about 7-8 minutes or until golden brown, turning them over half-way through if necessary. Top with cream gravy.

Cream Gravy

¹/₄   cup pan drippings
3   tablespoons flour
2   cups evaporated milk

1   cup unsalted beef stock
¹/₂   teaspoon pepper
Salt to taste

After frying steak, pour off top fat and leave about 1/4 cup of pan drippings in skillet. Place skillet over medium heat and sprinkle in flour, stirring to avoid lumps. Add evaporated milk and stock then simmer until liquid thickens, about 3 minutes. Stir gravy well and salt and pepper to taste.

Bubba Burgers

Everyone loves a good hamburger or cheeseburger. They're best done on the grill, but fried in the kitchen will do if it's cold or raining.

2	lbs lean ground meat (I like the flavor of chuck)	1/2	teaspoon cracked pepper
1	teaspoon garlic salt	8	slabs of Cheddar cheese

Work the garlic salt and pepper into the meat with your fingers. Make big thick patties for the grill. Make the center of your patties a little thinner than the outside of the patties for the purpose of cooking evenly. This little trick really helps! Grill your meat and cheese and put into toasted buns and set out the following:

Tomato slices   Sliced onion
Lettuce leaves   Mustard
Dill pickle slices   Mayonnaise (Sissy burger,
Chopped jalapeños   sissy burger!)

Try the steak fries in the this book to go with these burgers.

Serves 6.

Cowboys say . . .

"A hand that isn't there when you need it is like a big old blister. It only shows up when the work is done!"

Barbecue

Barbecue is a treasured staple food in the Lone Star State. We barbecue just about anything and everything! Steak, chicken, sausage, game, seafood, pork, ribs, weiners, burgers. Most Texans think of barbecue as smoked meat with a sauce, usually tomato based, as an accompaniment. We all have our own way of barbecuing or smoking meats. We pick the meat we like and "fire up the grill." We get the heat just right, using the wood taste we like and waiting until the perfect moment to "put the meat on." We season our meat with whatever dry spices suit our taste buds. Texans keep their barbecue sauce made up and in the refrigerator to take out and use at will. This is very convenient. I will share my "mop sop" with you.

For chicken, seafood and pork I use a good sprinkling of garlic salt, pepper and whatever I am in the mood for. For steak I use pepper, light lemon pepper, and garlic salt if I am not using a sauce. I do use a sauce most of the time, so I use a dry rub such as you will find elsewhere in this book. I cook my meat about three-fourths done and then I put sauce on both sides. I repeat this several times and let it caramelize on the meat. To get this caramel effect add about 2 tablespoons sugar to your dry rub for about each 2 steaks. Watch carefully – it tends to burn because of the sugar. When you take your meat off the grill, serve it with warm barbecue sauce.A great combination of meats for your family is a large link of sausage, a large sirloin, and a few burger patties. I think chicken breasts or halves and sausage make a good combination. Also, chicken and ribs make a great meal. Remember the weiners for the kids! Use your own judgement to please your family. To me a true Texas barbecue includes the following:

Barbecued meat with sauce
Potato salad
Baked or pinto beans
Cole slaw
Pickles
Onions
Bread
Cobbler or banana pudding

This is a Texas banquet! Bon appetit y'all!

Barbecue Sauce (Mop Sop)

1	44-oz. bottle thick ketchup	1	teaspoon small cracked pepper
1/4	cup vinegar		
1/2	can beer (water will do)	1 1/2	teaspoon garlic salt OR 3 cloves, minced
1	tablespoon lemon juice		
1	tablespoon prepared mustard	1	teaspoon onion salt OR 3 tablespoons grated onion
4	tablespoons margarine		
1	cup packed brown sugar	1/2	teaspoon chili powder
3	teaspoons liquid smoke	1/2	teaspoon paprika
1/4	cup Worcestershire sauce	1	teaspoon Tabasco
		1/4	teaspoon cumin

Just dump all ingredients in a large pot – stir – bring to a boil. Immediately lower heat so that your sauce will simmer. I simmer my sauce about an hour stirring occasionally – longer if not thick and dark enough.

Keep Your Powder Dry Rub

1/4	cup chili powder	1	tablespoon garlic salt
3	tablespoons cumin	1	teaspoon cayenne
3	tablespoons paprika	1	teaspoon dry mustard
2	tablespoons cracked pepper	2	teaspoons sugar
1	tablespoon oregano		

This is hot, no doubt about it. Texans love hot things, or most Texans do.

Sprinkle your rub on the first time you use it. Use it more liberally after that if desired. Use this on beef, chicken and pork before grilling it.

Texans use a rub and then a sauce after cooking or later in the cooking process. You can keep this rub made up and in a sealed jar. It lasts forever. You might die before it does.

Southern Fried Catfish

2	lbs. catfish fillets		2	teaspoons paprika
2	cups buttermilk		2	teaspoons salt
2-3	teaspoon Tabasco		1	teaspoon black pepper
1	garlic clove, minced			Cayenne to taste
1/2	cup cornmeal, medium-grind			Oil for frying
1/2	cup cornmeal, extra-fine-grind			

Soak catfish fillets in buttermilk, Tabasco and garlic. Refrigerate at least one hour. Combine cornmeals, paprika, salt, pepper and cayenne in a shallow bowl. Pour oil in skillet, enough to go half way up your fillets. Heat oil to 350° F. Drain fillets and coat in cornmeal on both sides. Fry fillets about 5 minutes per 1/2-inch thickness, turning once. Drain fillets and serve immediately with lemon wedges, tartar sauce, catsup, or Tabasco.

Serves 6.

Sauce Diane

1/2	cup butter		1	tablespoon lemon juice
2	teaspoons dry mustard		1	tablespoon Worcestershire
3/4	lb. sliced mushrooms		1/2	teaspoon salt
1	cup chopped green onions		1/2	teaspoon cracked pepper
3	cloves garlic, minced		1/4	cup chopped parsley OR 1 tablespoon dried parsley

Melt butter; stir in mustard, mushrooms, onions, and garlic. Saute 8 minutes. Stir in all other ingredients.

This is a great sauce for grilled steak or grilled chicken breast.

King Ranch Chicken Casserole

A real Texas favorite.

SAUCE

2	tablespoons unsalted butter
2	garlic cloves, minced
1/4	teaspoon ground dried red chile

Pinch ground cumin

2	tablespoons flour
3/4	cup unsalted chicken stock
1/2	cup milk
2	tablespoons sour cream

Salt and pepper to taste

FILLING

1	tablespoon unsalted butter
1/2	medium onion, chopped
1/2	medium green bell pepper, chopped
1/4	cup roasted green chile, chopped
6	oz. mushrooms, finely chopped
1/2	cup diced tomatoes

2	tablespoons pimientos

Oil for frying

8	corn tortillas
2-3	cups cooked chicken, diced
1 1/2	cups grated mild Cheddar cheese
1/4	cup sliced green onions

Preheat oven to 350° F. and grease large baking dish. Melt butter in medium skillet and add garlic, chile and cumin. Sauté 1-2 minutes, sprinkle with flour, and stir. Pour in chicken stock and milk, stirring constantly. Simmer about 3 minutes or until thickened. Stir in sour cream, salt and pepper, then set sauce aside.

Melt butter in skillet for filling. Add all ingredients and sauté. Heat about 1/2-inch oil in small skillet, then dunk totillas in oil, using tongs, a couple of times in order to soften them. Layer half the tortillas and chicken, a third of the sauce and half each of filling, cheese and onions in baking dish. Spoon on another third of sauce, then repeat layering, ending with the remainder of the sauce. Bake 30 minutes or until bubbly.

Serves 6-8.

★

Chicken & Dumplings

1	large stewing hen OR 4 chicken breasts	1/3	cup water
		Salt and pepper to taste	
2	cans chicken broth	1	stalk celery
2	cans water	1	carrot
4	tablespoons flour	1	small onion

Boil chicken with 1 stalk celery, 1 carrot and 1 small onion. Throw away vegetables and make bit-sized pieces of chicken to put back into the pot when dumplings are done. Some people like the vegetables finely chopped and put back also. Whatever floats your boat. I simmer my chicken and vegetables for about 1-1/2 hours. After removing chicken and vegetables, whisk flour into 1/3 cup water and stir into broth. Bring to a simmer and slowly drop dumplings into the pot one at a time slowly. Simmer about 25 minutes covered, stir and add chicken back to pot.

Dumplings

2	cups flour	1	tablespoon butter
1	teaspoon salt	2/3	cup milk
3/4	teaspoon baking powder		

Sift dry ingredients together. Cut in butter. Stir in milk. Roll out on floured board. Cut into 2-inch strips.

Serves 6-8

Bubba says . . .

"Walk tall and keep your head high, unless you're in a cow pasture that is."

★

Texas Sheet Cake

We Texans know to say "sheathcake" but most of us don't. Whatever you call it it's the best chocolate cake ever, still. I keep trying to find a better one, but simply cannot!

In a bowl:

2	cups flour	1/2	teaspoon salt
2	cups sugar	2	eggs, beaten
1	teaspoon baking soda	1/2	cup buttermilk
1	teaspoon vanilla		

In a saucepan, bring to a boil:
2   sticks margarine
4   tablespoons cocoa
1   cup water

Pour the contents of the saucepan over the flour ingredients in the bowl. Mix well and pour into an 11 x 16-inch greased pan. Bake 20-25 minutes or until done at a preheated 350° F.

Icing

1	stick margarine	6 tablespoons milk
4	tablespoons cocoa	

Bring to a boil and quickly stir and remove from heat

In a large bowl:

1	1-lb box powdered sugar	1	teaspoon vanilla
1	cup chopped pecans		

Pour hot mixture over sugar. Add vanilla and stir. Add pecans and stir. Pour over barely warm cake.

★

Pecan Pie

Texans love pie and they love Texas pecans, so it's a natural assumption they love pecan pie. Right! Now let's pronounce pecan, it's "pah-con" in Texas. Pēcan belongs under your grandmother's bed and don't forget it.

3	beaten eggs		1	teaspoon vanilla
3/4	cup sugar		1	cup chopped pecans
3/4	cup white Karo		1/8	teaspoon salt
3	tablespoons melted butter		8-inch pie crust	
1	teaspoon white vinegar			

Thoroughly mix all ingredients together. Pour into an unbaked pie shell. Bake in a preheated 375° F. oven about 30 minutes or until knife comes out clean.

Buttermilk Pie

This is my Texas favorite pie. I can't think of a more delicious end to a meal than this inexpensive delight! It makes 2 8-inch pies, so make someone's day and give them a gift of the other pie. It also freezes well.

This recipe is all done by hand. It's a one bowl, one spoon recipe. Easy cleanup!

3 3/4	cup sugar		2	teaspoons vanilla
1/3	cup flour		1	tablespoon lemon juice
1/2	teaspoon salt		1 3/4	sticks melted margarine OR butter
6	beaten eggs			
1	cup buttermilk			

In a large bowl, mix sugar, flour and salt together with a whisk. Whisk in eggs, buttermilk, vanilla and lemon juice. Whisk well for one minute. Add the melted margarine and whisk until margarine disappears into the batter completely. Pour into 2 8-inch pie shells and place in a preheated 375° F. oven for approximately 50 minutes or until set. Remove from oven and cool on racks.

Rice Pudding

You'll love this inexpensive, delicious dessert.

3	cups cooked rice	$2^1/4$	teaspoons vanilla
$1^1/4$	cup sugar	$1/16$	teaspoon almond extract
2	tablespoons melted butter	$1/8$	teaspoon cinnamon
4	large OR 5 medium eggs	$1/8$	teaspoon nutmeg
$1^1/4$	cup milk	1	cup raisins
$1/4$	teaspoon salt		

TOPPING

$1/3$	cup packed brown sugar	2	tablespoons melted butter

PUDDING

Whisk eggs. Add all ingredients except raisins and whisk again. Stir in raisins and pour into a heavily buttered baking dish about 8- or 10-inches round and deep. Butter dish with 1/2 the melted butter and put the other half into the pudding. Bake 375° F. 20 minutes. Lower temperature to 350° F. and bake another 20 minutes. Evenly spread the brown sugar over the custard, then evenly drizzle the butter over and bake another 5-8 minutes.

Serves 8-12.

Cowboys say . . .

"No matter where you ride, there you are!"

★

My Mother's Banana Pudding

3/4	cup sugar	1	tablespoon vanilla
3	tablespoons cornstarch		Cream of tartar
3	egg yolks, beaten		Vanilla wafers
	(save the whites)	4	bananas
2	cups milk		

Preheat oven to 425° F. Add 1/4 cup sugar and pinch of cream of tarter to 3 egg whites. Beat until stiff peaks form and set aside. Mix the first five ingredients together in a saucepan over medium heat, stirring constantly until custard thickens. Remove from heat and layer bottom of baking dish with custard. Next, place a layer of vanilla wavers atop custard and a layer of sliced bananas atop the wafers, then cover with custard. Repeat layering, then put one more layer of wafers and custard on top. Cover with meringue and bake 5-8 minutes or until golden brown. If you don't like meringue, put wafers on top.

Serves 4-6.

Old Fashioned
Homemade Vanilla Ice Cream

6	eggs	13	oz. evaporated milk
2	cups sugar	1	gallon whole milk
1/4	teaspoon salt		Ice
1	tablespoon vanilla		Rock salt

In a large mixing bowl, beat eggs. Gradually add sugar, stirring constantly. Add salt, vanilla and evaporated milk. Add about a pint of the fresh milk and mix.

Pour mixture into ice cream freezer and add enough of the remainder of the milk to fill can to the middle of the top board of dasher.

Assemble the ice cream freezer. Add chipped ice and rock salt to barrel around freezer can. Crank freezer until ice cream begins to freeze, adding more ice and salt, as needed. When handle becomes difficult to turn, remove turning mechanism, and carefully remove top from freezer can and remove dasher. Replace top and cover can with more ice and salt. Cover ice with old towel for at least 1 hour.

Nana's Sweet Potato Pies

4	cups mashed sweet potatoes		Dash salt
2	cups milk	4	eggs, large
2	cups sugar	1	teaspoon cinnamon
1	tablespoon vanilla	1/4	teaspoon nutmeg
1/2	stick butter, melted		

Beat all ingredients 3-4 minutes. Pour into two unbaked pie crust. Bake 350° F. for 50 to 60 minutes, or until custard is set and brown spots start to appear on tops of pies.

Cherry Cobbler

2	cans sour cherries with juice minus 1/4 cup	1/8	teaspoon salt
1/3	cup flour	1/4	teaspoon cinnamon
1 1/4	cup sugar	2	tablespoons melted butter

Mix flour, sugar, cinnamon and salt together. Add cherries and juice, reserving 1/4 cup. Add melted butter. Stir well and pour into a prepared cobbler crust in an 8 x 8-inch pan. Use the cobbler crust for peach cobbler in this book, but only 1/2 of it. Or you can use half and freeze half. Bake 350° F. approximately 50 minutes. The reserved juice can be added back to the cobbler the next day.

Cowboys say . . .

"A really god friend will ride with you 'til hell freezes over and a little farther on the ice."

★

Lisa's Green Bean Casserole

2   cans French style
green beans, drained
1   tablespoon margarine
1   can cream of
mushroom soup
1/2   cup milk
2   teaspoons dried onion

1/8   teaspoon pepper
1   cup grated Cheddar
cheese
1/4   cup Parmesan cheese
1   can onion rings
NO SALT

Drain the green beans and place 2/3 of them into a buttered (I use margarine) 8 x 8-inch ovenproof dish. Top it evenly with the Cheddar cheese. Place soup in a bowl and beat in the milk, onion salt and pepper until smooth. Pour 1/2 of this mixture evenly over cheese. Put remaining green beans into the casserole and spread. Pour the rest of the soup mixture over the green beans.

Sprinkle Parmesan cheese over the entire casserole top. Bake at 350° F. for 30 minutes. Take out and top with onion rings and bake another 8-10 minutes or until onion rings are crunchy.

Bubba says . . .

"If you have an itch for something, you'd better have the scratch too!"

Acknowledgements

The best that any cook or reader of a cookbook, or author of a cookbook can do is gather recipes from far and wide, from friends and enemies, from newspapers, books and magazines, restaurants, churches, organizations, dinner parties, bridge clubs and I could go on for pages. I have been collecting recipes for many years. All we can do as cooks to make a recipe truly ours is to "make it up" and change an existing recipe to suit us. Most of my recipes are "made up," but some have been around for ages.

I would love to give credit where credit is due, but simply cannot as I don't know or remember. However, I do thank all of you who have in any way contributed to this book or my recipe collection.

Index

Appetizers (Whore's d'oeuvres)

Soups & Salads (Slurps & Burps)

Bread   (Bread, Butter & "Honey")

Main Dishes   (The Whole Hogg)

Vegetable & Side Dishes   (True Grits)

Wild Game Recipes

Desserts   (Real Sweet)

Diane's Lone Star Legacies

NOTES

NOTES

Texas Cookie Cutters

Order the "best cookies in Texas" (and that's the world!) straight from Deep in the Heart of Texas. Mix & Match your flavors. The cookies are Texas sized, soft and chewy and to die for! Did I mention "to die for"?

Please Choose from and Specify No. of Pastries requested.

COOKIES TO DIE FOR

_____ Chocolate Chip
_____ Chocolate Chip Pecan
_____ White Chocolate, Macadamia
_____ White Chocolate, Almond & Toffee
_____ Almond Chocolate Crunch
_____ Pecan Crunch
_____ Peanut butter
_____ Peanut butter Chip
_____ Oatmeal Raisin
_____ Oatmeal Raisin, Chocolate Chip
_____ Old Fashioned Sugar
_____ Tipple Chocolate Bon Bons

1 Dz. Cookies $ 9.75 + $4.00
     Packing Charge _____
2 Dz. Cookies $19.95 + $4.50
     Packing Charge _____
Gift Wraps, Please add
     $3.00 each item _____
Gift Baskets, add $10.00 for
1 dozen – $18.00 for 2 dozen _____

OUR OWN CAKES & BARS

_____ 10" Chocolate Pound Cake w/Drizzle
    $18.00
_____ 10" Lemon Pound Cake w/Drizzle
    $18.00
_____ 10" Rum Cake w/Drizzle
    $18.00
_____ 1 Dozen. Raspberry Oatbran Bars
    $15.00
_____ 1 Dozen Cream Cheese Brownies
    $15.00

Cakes , ea. $18.00 + $4.00
     Packing Charge _____
Oatbran Bars, dz. $15.00 + $4.00
     Packing Charge _____
Brownies, dz. $15.00 + $4.00
     Packing Charge _____

Gift Wrap $3.00 each item _____

TOTAL ORDER   _____

We will charge you ONLY the actual cost of shipping your cookies wherever you wish to ship. We will need a Credit Card Number and Expiration Date to process this order.

These cookies are the best gifts ever. Trust me.   Please send above to (print):

Name _____

Address _____

City _____ State_____ Zip _____

Charge to ❑ Visa ❑ MasterCard ❑ American Express

Card No. _____ Exp. Date _____ / _____ / _____

Please mail your order to: **Texas Cookie Cutters**
c/o Diane Gregg
2034 Verbena Drive • Austin, TX 78750

Order Your Bubba Basics

Every T-Shirt and Cap has a large shape of Texas with a message inside it. The cap says "BUBBA" across the shape of Texas. Our shirts and caps are very good quality.

BUBBA SAYS T-SHIRTS . . . . $18.00 EACH
Plus $6.00 Shipping & Handling

BUBBA CAPS . . . . $14.00 EACH
Plus $4.00 Shipping & Handling

Please Specify No. of Items Requested

No.	Message	Price	TOTAL
_____	BUBBA SAYS "I FEAR NO BEER"	$18.00 EA	_____
_____	BUBBA SAYS "SECEDE"	$18.00 EA	_____
_____	BUBBA SAYS "DRIVE 90, FREEZE A YANKEE"	$18.00 EA	_____
_____	BUBBA SAYS "I BRAKE FOR ARMADILLOS"	$18.00 EA	_____
_____	BUBBA SAYS "GOD BLESS TEXAS"	$18.00 EA	_____
_____	BUBBA CAP (Circle one; Red Blue)	$14.00 EA	_____
_____	BUBBA CAP (with either shirt above) (Shipping & Handling 6.00)	$29.95 EA	_____

BUBBA CAP HAS "BUBBA" ON IT OVER THE SHAPE OF TEXAS

Shipping & Handling _____

Gift Wraps, Please add $3.00 each item _____

Texans please add sales tax (.0825%) to your order _____

TOTAL ORDER _____

Please send above to (print): _____

Name _____

Address _____

City _____   State _____ Zip _____

Make check payable to: Diane Gregg
                              2034 Verbena Drive
                              Austin, TX 78750

O R D E R   F O R M

Order Your Texas "Dry Rub Tub"

Straight from Deep in the Heart of Texas. It comes in a 2-cup tub ready to sprinkle on your favorite meat for a delicious taste treat. You can order:

2-Cup Tub of Texas Dry Rub $9.95 EACH
                                               Plus $4.00 Shipping & Handling

Send as a gift to someone and we'll give it a real Texas gift wrap for $3.00 more. Great gifts! You'll know it's from Texas!

Extra Special Texas Deal – Order for yourself or send to a special person *The Bubba Does Texas Cookbook* + the Texas Rub Tub for a special price of $27.50. We will gift wrap for free. Add $6.00 shipping and handling.

Please Specify No. of Items Requested

No.	Item	Price	TOTAL
_____	**AMATEUR (Spicy, but not too hot)**	$ 9.95 EA	_____
_____	**RIDIN' THE FENCE (Bold & hot)**	$ 9.95 EA	_____
_____	**REAL TEXAS (Hotter'n Texas in July)**	$ 9.95 EA	_____
_____	**COOKBOOK & TUB OF RUB**	$27.00 EA	_____
	(Circle 1 – Amateur Ridin' the Fence Real Texas		

Shipping & Handling

Gift Wraps, Please add $3.00 each item   _____

Texans please add sales tax (.0825%) to your order   _____

TOTAL ORDER   _____

Please send above to (print):

Name _____

Address _____

City _____ State _____ Zip _____

Make check payable to: **Diane Gregg**
                                2034 Verbena Drive
                                Austin, TX 78750

The Bubba Does Texas Cookbook

c/o Diane Gregg
2034 Verbena Dr.
Austin, TX 78750

Please send _____ copies of **Bubba Does Texas Cookbook** @ $19.95 each _____

Postage & Handling $3.50 each _____

Gift wrap $3.00 each _____

Texas residents Texas Sales Tax $1.89 each _____

TOTAL _____

Name _____

Address _____

City _____ State_____ Zip _____

Make checks payable to Diane Gregg.

The Bubba Does Texas Cookbook

c/o Diane Gregg
2034 Verbena Dr.
Austin, TX 78750

Please send _____ copies of **Bubba Does Texas Cookbook** @ $19.95 each _____

Postage & Handling $3.50 each _____

Gift wrap $3.00 each _____

Texas residents Texas Sales Tax $1.89 each _____

TOTAL _____

Name _____

Address _____

City _____ State_____ Zip _____

Make checks payable to Diane Gregg.

ORDER FORM